D1106866

EDUCATION IN THE NEW AGE

BOOKS BY ALICE A. BAILEY

EDUCATION IN THE NEW AGE

by

ALICE A. BAILEY

LUCIS PUBLISHING COMPANY
New York

LUCIS PRESS LTD.
London

The publication of this book is financed by the Tibetan Book Fund which is established for the perpetuation of the teachings of the Tibetan and Alice A. Bailey.

This Fund is controlled by the Lucis Trust, a tax-exempt, religious, educational corporation.

The Lucis Publishing Company is a non-profit organisation owned by the Lucis Trust. No royalties are paid on this book.

This title is also avaible in Dutch, Spanish, German and Italian. Translation into other languages is proceeding.

MANUFACTURED IN THE UNITED STATES OF AMERICA
By Fort Orange Press, Inc., Albany, N. Y.

PREFACE

This book on educational philosophy comes at a time of crisis, for the theme that runs through critical thinking in the field of educational theory today is characterized by deep concern over both the preservation and the enrichment of human values. Can we maintain our democratic individualism in the face of the standardizing forces of the Western machine civilization which may also engulf the Eastern world? Can we offset the totalitarianisms which deify the materialism of an increasingly industrial culture?

In May of this year (1953) I attended a two-day seminar in Chicago, sponsored by *The Center for the Study of Liberal Education for Adults,* a subdivision of the Ford Foundation, created to express the growing concern of our times for the spiritual basis of our civilization. In the statement of the problem which our group was to study, *Education in a Democratic Society,* we were informed as follows:

"Education must meet the needs of the human spirit. It must assist persons to develop a satisfactory personal philosophy and sense of values; to cultivate tastes for literature, music and the arts; to grow in ability to analyze problems and arrive at thoughtful conclusions."

This statement demands a re-examination of our educational theory and practice. A survey of current developments proves that, at long last, the professional educators *are* clarifying a common philosophy and *are* consciously striving to delineate a theory of education adequate to the new world that is emerging. In such a philosophy three fundamental needs must be met: (1) *a psychological theory* of the human person to be "educated"; (2) *a social theory* of the kind of

v

society one is trying to create or preserve as a suitable home for the cultural ideals promulgated; and (3) *a world view or cosmology,* a theory of man's place in the universe in which man is spectator and actor.

Our problem is to attain the kind of overall synthesis that Marxism and neo-Scholasticism provide for their followers, but to get this by the freely chosen cooperative methods that Dewey advocated. In the broadest terms such a world-view will make possible a planetary civilization by integrating whatever trans-temporal and trans-spatial truths about man and the universe we can extract from all regional cultures in their local times and places. These universal principles will then provide the norms for *Education in the New Age,* as the Tibetan terms it.

The world today suffers from a cultural provincialism based on the dualism of an outward-looking, objective attitude of the Western world, and an inwardness or subjectivity of Oriental societies. Each of these civilizations, in its extreme form, is over-balanced in its own direction. In harmonious living, man must integrate both ideals to achieve wholeness for himself and his world. This, it seems to me, is one important theme of the present work.

For the future, the remedy for the social schisms and psychological fissions that have handicapped and obstructed our modern efforts to overcome the divisions of humanity, lies in a restoration of *unity of principles* upon which an integration of human values and achievements can be attempted. The educational implications of this development are clear. As the Tibetan indicates, on subjective levels we must provide for the resynthesis of human personality and for the overcoming of the double consciousness that has resulted from the cultural fission which made the "self-negation" of the peaceful civilization of the Orient the overpowering concept of its culture, and the aggressive "individualism" of the Occident the ideal of Western man. Accordingly, we need not only the political synthesis of a

World Federation in which the Eastern and Western hemispheres function like the right and left lobes of man's brain, with the seat of the World Brain serving as the point of decussation of the planetary nerves, but we need also a planetary way of life, a planetary ethics, and a planetary way of feeling to supply the powerful drive we shall require for the great tasks that lie ahead of us.

The time to resynthesize the objective and subjective, the extrovert and the introvert civilizations and to achieve a great orchestration of culture *is now*. Japan was not aggressive until the country learned the trick from the West. Before her doors were forced, her arts and philosophy were in tune with oriental tradition. When she adopted Western technology, she threw overboard her ancient culture. What happened in Japan can happen in the rest of the Orient, but whereas Japan was a relatively small country, China, India and their neighbors are vast and populous. Heaven help us if they re-enact the history of Japan. Our activity in the resynthesizing of the world must include, through our own efforts to understand and appreciate, an appeal to the Orient to preserve and develop the fundamental values in its regional cultures. While the West is seeking the principles upon which peaceful and fruitful living can be founded, the East may provide us with the counter-balance to our aggressive materialism.

If this new synthesis is to restore cultural and spiritual unity in mankind, the Occidental world will have to acquire humility when it turns to the Orient. The Oriental world will not, because of its inherent nature, generate the physical energy to go to the West. We Westerners went into the East in search of markets—outlets for the products of our mechanical power—and we must return to our own world, magnetized by the subjective energies of the East and conscious of it. Our aggressive commercial penetration of Oriental lands and peoples has had the end result of bringing the literature, the philosophy and the arts of the East into the

West as uncalculated dividends. We can, if we choose, make use of the vast heritage of Oriental culture available to us, even in our neighborhood libraries.

Our main hope of survival in this highly polarized world lies in a prodigious effort at synthesis of the two cultures *while there is still time.* Should the Orient deny us that time and decide to meet us merely on our own grounds, then this might write *finis* to the story for all of us, East and West.

During our industrial and expansionist age there have been increasing evidences of the permeating power of Oriental thought in the fields of science, philosophy and the arts of the West. Psychosomatic medicine, parapsychology, Jung's analytical psychology are only a few indications of contemporary inwardly-oriented researches. The re-entry of the spiritual factor in life and education is something more than a recrudescence of some earlier forms of Christian ideology.

In this education for the New Age, the type of East-West philosophy presented by the Tibetan will find its proper setting. Here we have the elements of a complete theory, as follows:

  (a) *Subjective Planning*; a theory of the creative self-development of the individual.
  (b) *Objective Planning*; a theory of the good society for human persons to live in.

The psychological and social implications of the education for the New Age must be stated as explicitly as possible. The next step is to test the validity of the principles in concrete applications. The testing must be done in terms of operational techniques relevant to the Hindu psychology, rather than by Western positivistic procedures. Until this program has been given a fair trial, it is a waste of time to attempt to prejudge the issue. Yet it is not necessary to consider the ancient East and the modern West approaches as two mutually exclusive alternatives. In some instances the approaches are merely two "languages" for stating universal truths about human nature and we are not faced with an either-or antithesis. Intertranslation may reduce the strangeness of terminology. For example, the Tibetan's view that "meditation is thinking things through" is good Dewey doctrine. As the elements of unfamiliarity diminish, understanding is facilitated.

That the research project so briefly sketched is not some vague philosophical phantasy but an urgent and immediate need is indicated by a document drawn up by the Department for Cultural Activities of UNESCO which formulated the theme for discussion in these terms: "The Concept of Man and the Philosophy of Education in East and West." Here it is stated:

"Unesco could not remain indifferent to this problem (of East and West); it was bound to face it squarely in the present circumstances of the world, brought about by the increasingly rapid process of unification, the reduction of distances, the growing importance of technology, the gradual attainment by all peoples of political independence and international responsibility and, above all, the disquiet and perplexity prevailing among the *two* great civilizations of yesterday, ready to give birth to the *one* civilization of tomorrow but cowering under the threat of a world crisis far beyond their capacity to control."

In an article on *Our Goal Is Unity* in *The Free World* of October, 1944, Dr. Albert Einstein regretfully took note of "an odious materialistic attitude toward life which leads to the predominance of an unrestrained selfishness." But how shall this materialism and selfishness of our culture be corrected? By geodesies in the space-time manifold of relativity theory? This would be cold comfort from a warm heart and Einstein does not offer this way out. Indeed, Einstein offers no clear solution. The simple truth is that the only counterweight to "materialism" is "idealism" and this must come out of the very heart of science, as an evolutionary development. Researchers who know the data of science must take our knowledge about nature and synthesize it into a body of integrated principles to establish the Pythagorean-Platonic-Bruno cosmology, a world picture similar to the pantheism of Eastern thought, wherein man can reverence nature because nature is worthy of awe and reverence. A humanism that is exclusively anthropocentric is over-balanced and is in need of a world philosophy in which the infinite and eternal cosmos yields the other pivot for the axis around which the new synthesis can move and grow.

There is a remedy for "the sickness of modern man" and many of its constituents are found in this book on the education of the future. The implementation of the principles involved is the work of humanity itself. That its theories are not beyond the need and grasp of contemporary educationists is borne out by the fact that steps are already taken in several places for the setting up of experiments in education which are to express the need for synthesis. As an example of this development there is the "self-survey" project financed by the Ford Foundation out of which has come a proposal for a Department of Integrating Studies in the University of Pittsburgh. Part of the statement presenting this experiment reads as follows:

"It has been proposed that a new department, *outside* the present three distribution fields of the Humanities, the Social Sciences and the Natural Sciences, and different from the departments *within* existing distribution fields, be established at the University of Pittsburgh. This new department shall be termed the Department of Unified Studies. It shall be concerned with seeking the interrelationships between various subject matter disciplines already available in the offerings of the University. The main objective is to cultivate the habit of reflective synthesis and find or create a body of wisdom for human evolution and personal self-development.

"Since unified interpretation and understanding is not a science in its own right but a synoptic comprehension of antecedent bodies of concepts and principles, this department shall not offer degrees in its own area or 'field.' The Department of Unified Studies is primarily a service department to the students and faculty members carrying on their primary (but not more important) activities in the more specialized areas of study.

"Until contemporary times, there has been little need for such an adjunct to our institutions of higher learning. But with the increase in size of our specialized bodies of knowledge—to the point where we are burying ourselves under the mountains of information and data—the time has come to take seriously the problem of finding out what all this knowledge means. If the University cannot synthesize the overall implications of modern learning it will abdicate its historic role of providing universal principles for enlightened individuals seeking the benefits of the good life. This urgent need here requires explicit statement and recognition, if we are consciously to design a solution to the problem.

"The broad purpose of the *Advancement of Learning* (to use Bacon's phrase) is to throw light on four basic questions of human existence:

(1) What is man?
(2) What kind of physical universe (cosmos) is it that man inhabits?
(3) By what processes of evolution did the human species emerge from the matrix of nature so that man could become the self-conscious and creative individual he now is?
(4) Knowing something about the cosmos and about human nature, what is the best kind of society for man's progressive self-evolution?

"In seeking answers to these questions and providing students with the stimuli and data necessary to the formulation of their own answers, the instructors in the Department of Unified Studies will not pose as experts in integration. Along with interested students, the faculty members will be *seekers after synthesis*. To illustrate the type of courses contemplated, the following possibilities are suggested:

1. The Sociology of Knowledge.
2. The Interrelationships of Religion, Philosophy, Science and Art.
3. Information Theory, Cybernetics and Semantics.
4. The History and Philosophy of Science.
5. The History and Presuppositions of the Democratic Theory of Government (Ideology).
6. Contributions of Biology, Sociology and Psychiatry to Human Welfare and Progress.
7. The Unity of Knowledge.
8. The Evolution of Value Systems from Primitive Culture to Modern Industrial Civilization.

"The first prerequisites of all such courses is that they shall interrelate not less than three so-called departments of study. Thus the students and faculty will be encouraged to search for vision—'seeing life steadily and as a whole.' "

The Tibetan's seed-principles will find prepared soil in such experimental fields.

OLIVER L. REISER

Department of Philosophy
University of Pittsburgh
Pittsburgh, Pennsylvania
U.S.A.

EXTRACT FROM A STATEMENT BY THE TIBETAN

PUBLISHED AUGUST 1934

Suffice it to say, that I am a Tibetan disciple of a certain degree, and this tells you but little, for all are disciples from the humblest aspirant up to, and beyond, the Christ Himself. I live in a physical body like other men, on the borders of Tibet, and at times (from the exoteric standpoint) preside over a large group of Tibetan lamas, when my other duties permit. It is this fact that has caused it to be reported that I am an abbot of this particular lamasery. Those associated with me in the work of the Hierarchy (and all true disciples are associated in this work) know me by still another name and office. A.A.B. knows who I am and recognises me by two of my names.

I am a brother of yours, who has travelled a little longer upon the Path than has the average student, and has therefore incurred greater responsibilities. I am one who has wrestled and fought his way into a greater measure of light than has the aspirant who will read this article, and I must therefore act as a transmitter of the light, no matter what the cost. I am not an old man, as age counts among the teachers, yet I am not young or inexperienced. My work is to teach and spread the knowledge of the Ageless Wisdom wherever I can find a response, and I have been doing this for many years. I seek also to help the Master M. and the Master K.H. whenever opportunity offers, for I have been long connected with Them and with Their work. In all the above, I have told you much; yet at the same time I have told you nothing which would lead you to offer me that blind obedience and the foolish devotion which the emotional aspirant offers to the Guru and Master Whom he is as yet unable to contact. Nor will he make that desired contact until he has transmuted emotional devotion into unselfish service to humanity—not to the Master.

The books that I have written are sent out with no claim for their acceptance. They may, or may not, be correct, true and useful. It is for you to ascertain their truth by right practice and by the exercise of the intuition. Neither I nor A. A. B. is the least interested in having them acclaimed as inspired writings, or in having anyone speak of them (with bated breath) as being the work of one of the Masters. If they present truth in such a way that it follows sequentially upon that already offered in the world teachings, if the information given raises the aspiration and the will-to-serve from the plane of the emotions to that of the mind (the plane whereon the Masters *can* be found) then they will have served their purpose. If the teaching conveyed calls forth a response from the illumined mind of the worker in the world, and brings a flashing forth of his intuition, then let that teaching be accepted. But not otherwise. If the statements meet with eventual corroboration, or are deemed true under the test of the Law of Correspondences, then that is well and good. But should this not be so, let not the student accept what is said.

TABLE OF CONTENTS

CHAPTER I

The Objective of the New Education

INTRODUCTORY STATEMENTS

THIS PRESENTATION might be regarded as concerning itself with three different aspects of one general theme, which is that of the new and coming educational methods and ideas. The objective is to elucidate the cultural unfoldment of the race and to consider the next step to be taken in the mental development of humanity. Teaching, if true, must be in line with the past and must provide scope for endeavour in the present and must also hold out further enlightenment for those who have succeeded or are succeeding in attaining the indicated goals. There must be a spiritual future indicated. It is that which is required now.

The word "spiritual" does not refer to religious matters, so-called. All activity which drives the human being forward towards some form of development—physical, emotional, mental, intuitional, social—if it is in advance of his present state is essentially spiritual in nature and is indicative of the livingness of the inner divine entity. The spirit of man is undying; it forever endures, progressing from point to point and stage to stage upon the Path of Evolution, unfolding steadily and sequentially the divine attributes and aspects.

The three points of our general theme are:

1. *The Technique of the Education of the Future.*
2. *The Science of the Antahkarana.* This deals with the mode of bridging the gap which exists in man's consciousness between the world of ordinary human experience, the threefold world of physical-emotional-mental functioning, and the higher levels of so-called spiritual development which is the world of ideas, of intuitive perception, of spiritual insight and understanding.
3. *Methods of Building the Antahkarana.* This leads to the overcoming of the limitations—physical and psychological—which restrict man's free expression of his innate divinity. Here we can only prepare the ground for this third point because the subject involves advanced meditation practices which must be approached gradually. I have dealt with meditation in my other books.

The question might here be asked, why it is of value to consider giving time to that which lies as yet in the future. I would reply by reminding you that "As a man thinketh, so is he." This is a truism and a platitude of occultism. Therefore, what is true of the individual is also true of the group and as a group thinks, so does it eventually react. As the group thought-waves penetrate into the mental atmosphere of humanity, men become impressed and the inaugurating of the new ways of living and of developing proceeds with increased facility. Here I seek only to give you some brief and general ideas which will serve to indicate to you the trend of my thought and the purpose which I have in mind. Perhaps the easiest way for me to do this is to formulate certain propositions which are of interest and which can carry illumination.

I. Education, up to the present time, has been occupied with the art of synthesising past history, past achievement in all departments of human thought and with the attainments to date of human knowledge. It has dealt with those forms of science which the past has evolved. It is primarily backward-looking and not forward-looking. I would remind you that I am here generalising, and that there are many and notable small exceptions to this attitude.

II. Education has concerned itself primarily with the organising of the lower mind, and a child's calibre has been largely gauged by its reaction to accumulated information (where education is concerned), collated and collected data, sequentially handed out, digested and arranged so as to equip the child to compete with the information which other people possess.

III. Education to date has been largely memory training, though there is now emerging the recognition that this attitude must end. The child has to assimilate the facts that the race believes to be true, has tested in the past and found adequate. But each age has a differing standard of adequacy. The Piscean Age dealt with the detail of the endeavour to measure up to a sensed ideal. Hence we have a history which covers the method whereby tribes acquired national status through aggression, war and conquest. That has been indicative of racial achievement.

Geography has been based on a similar reaction to an idea of expansion, and through it the child learns how men, driven by economic and other necessities, have conquered territory and absorbed lands. This too has been regarded, and rightly so, as a racial achievement. The various branches of science are also regarded as constituting the conquest of areas of territory, and this again is acclaimed as racial achievement. The conquests of science, the conquests of nations, and the conquests of territory are all indicative of the Piscean method, with its idealism, its militancy, and its separativeness in all fields—religious, political and economic. But the age of synthesis, of inclusiveness and of understanding is upon us, and the new education of the

Aquarian Age must begin very gently to penetrate the human aura.

IV. Education is more than memory training and more than informing a child or student as to the past and its achievements. Those factors have their place, and the past must be understood and studied, for out of it must grow that which is new, its flower and its fruit. Education involves more than the investigation of a subject and the forming of subsequent conclusions leading to hypotheses which, in their own turn, lead to still more investigation and conclusions. Education is more than a sincere effort to fit a child or adult to be a good citizen, an intelligent parent and no charge upon the state. It has a far wider application than producing a human being who will be a commercial asset and not a commercial liability. Education has other objectives than rendering life enjoyable and so enabling men and women to achieve a culture which will permit them to participate with interest in all that transpires in the three worlds of human affairs. It is all the above, but should also be much more.

V. Education has three major objectives, from the angle of human development:

First, as has been grasped by many, it must make a man an intelligent citizen, a wise parent, and a controlled personality; it must enable him to play his part in the work of the world and fit him for living peaceably and helpfully and in harmony with his neighbours.

Second, it must enable him to bridge the gap between the various aspects of his own mental nature, and herein lies the major emphasis of the instructions which I am now purposing to give you.

In the esoteric philosophy we are taught, as well you know, that on the mental plane there are three aspects of the mind, or of that mental creature we call a man. These three aspects constitute the most important part of his nature:

1. His lower concrete mind, the reasoning principle. It is with this aspect of the man that our educational processes profess to deal.
2. That Son of Mind, which we call the Ego or Soul. This is the intelligence principle, and is called by many names in the esoteric literature, such as the Solar Angel, the Agnishvattas, the Christ principle, etc. With this, religion in the past has professed to deal.
3. The higher abstract mind, the custodian of ideas, and that which is the conveyor of illumination to the lower mind, once that lower mind is en rapport with the soul. With this world of ideas philosophy has professed to deal.

We might call these three aspects:

The receptive mind, the mind as dealt with by the psychologists.
The individualised mind, the Son of Mind.
The illuminating mind, the higher mind.

Third, the gap between the lower mind and the soul has to be bridged, and curiously enough humanity has always realised this and has talked therefore in terms of "achieving unity" or "making the at-one-ment" or "attaining alignment." These are all attempts to express this intuitively realised truth.

VI. Education also should concern itself during the new age with the bridging of this gap between the three aspects of the mind nature: between the soul and the lower mind, thus producing at-one-ment between soul and personality; between the lower mind, the soul and the higher mind. For this the race is now ready, and for the first time in the career of humanity the bridging work can go forward on a relatively large scale. On this I need not enlarge, for it concerns the technicalities of the Ancient Wisdom, on which I have given you much in my other books.

VII. Education is therefore the Science of the Antah-karana. This science and this term is the esoteric way of expressing the truth of this bridging necessity. The antah-karana is the bridge the man builds—through meditation, understanding and the magical creative work of the soul—between the three aspects of his mind nature. Therefore, the primary objectives of the coming education will be:

1. To produce alignment between mind and brain through a correct understanding of the inner con-stitution of man, particularly of the etheric body and the force centres.
2. To build or construct a bridge between the brain-mind-soul, thus producing an integrated personality which is a steady developing expression of the in-dwelling soul.
3. To build the bridge between the lower mind, soul, higher mind, so that the illumination of the person-ality becomes possible.

VIII. The true education is consequently the science of linking up the integral parts of man, and also of linking him up in turn with his immediate environment, and then with the greater whole in which he has to play his part. Each aspect, regarded as a lower aspect, can ever be simply the expression of the next higher. In this phrase I have ex-pressed a fundamental truth which embodies not only the objective, but also indicates the problem before all in-terested in education. This problem is to gauge rightly the centre or the focus of a man's attention and to note where the consciousness is primarily centered. Then he must be trained in such a way that a shift of that focus into a higher vehicle becomes possible. We can also express this idea in an equally true manner by saying that the vehicle which seems of paramount importance can become and should become of secondary importance as it becomes simply the instrument of that which is higher than itself.

If the astral (emotional) body is the centre of the personality life, then the objective of the educational process imposed upon the subject will be to make the mind nature the dominating factor, and the astral body then becomes that which is impressed by, and is sensitive to, environing conditions, but is under the control of the mind. If the mind is the centre of personality attention, then the soul activity must be brought into fuller expression; and so on and on the work proceeds, progress being made from point to point until the top of the ladder has been reached.

It might be noted here that this entire exegesis of the mind and of the needed bridge building is but the practical demonstration of the truth of the occult aphorism that "before a man can tread the Path he must become that Path itself." The antahkarana is the Path symbolically. This is one of the paradoxes of the esoteric science. Step by step and stage by stage, we construct that Path just as the spider spins its thread. It is that "way back" which we evolve out of ourselves; it is that Way which we also find and tread.

Some Questions Answered

I will now attempt to deal somewhat with three questions on education asked by one of the students. I can but indicate the ideal, and in so doing I run the risk of producing an effect of being so visionary that any approach under our present system might be regarded as impossible.

In answer to the first question, the prime function of all educators is twofold:

1. To train the brain to respond intelligently to impressions coming to it via the sense apparatus and so carrying information about the outer tangible world.
2. To train the mind so that it can fulfill three duties:
   a. Deal intelligently with information relayed to it by the brain.

   b. Create thoughtforms in response to *impulses* emanating from the physical plane; to *emotional reactions* set in motion by the feeling-desire nature; to the *thought world,* in which the man's environment is found.
   c. Orient itself to the subjective spiritual self, so that, from a condition of potentiality, the self may emerge into active government.

In this formulation of the function of the apparatus with which all educators have to deal (the mind and the brain), I have indicated the answer to the second question asked, which was:

"Are there definite types of activities, changing with the growing years and based on the phases of the growth process in the individual, that make for his best all-around development?"

I differ somewhat concerning the periods indicated by such occult teachers as Steiner, for though the seven year cycles have their place, the division is apt to be over-applied. I would also suggest ten year cycles of development, divided into two parts: seven of learning and three of application.

In the first ten years of a child's life he is taught to deal intelligently with information coming to him via the five senses to the brain. Observation, rapid response, and physical coordination as the result of intention, must be emphasised. The child must be taught to hear and see, to make contacts and to use judgment; and his fingers must then respond to creative impulses to make and produce what he sees and hears. Thus are laid the elements of the arts and crafts, of drawing and of music.

In the next ten years the mind is definitely trained to become dominant. The child is taught to rationalise his emotional and desire impulses, and to discriminate the right from the wrong, the desirable from the undesirable, and the essential from the nonessential. This can be taught him through the medium of history and the intellectual training which the cycle of his life makes compulsory under the laws of the country in which he lives. A sense of values and of right standards is thus established. He is taught the distinction between memory training and thinking; between bodies of facts, ascertained by thinkers and tabulated in books, and their application to the events of objective existence, plus (and here lies a thought of real importance) their subjective cause and their relation to the world of reality of which the phenomenal world is but the symbol.

At the age of seventeen the study of psychology will be added to the rest of the curriculum and the nature of the soul and its relation to the World Soul will be investigated. Meditation along suitable lines will be part of the curriculum. It should be noted here, however, that the religious implications of meditation are needless. Meditation is the process whereby the objective tendencies and outgoing impulses of the mind are thwarted, and it begins to be subjective, to focus and to intuit. This can be taught through the medium of deep thinking on any subject—mathematics, biology, and so forth.

The tendency of the newer education should be to make the subject of the educational experiment the conscious possessor of his equipment; it should leave him standing clear-eyed before life, with open doors ahead of him into the world of objective phenomena and relationships; it should have brought him to the knowledge of a door leading into the world of Reality and through which he may pass at will and there assume and work out his relation to other souls.

This second question—relating to the type of experience which would aid the child to round out his development and be supplementary to the compulsory state curriculum—is well-nigh impossible to answer, owing to the wide differences in human beings and the practical impossibility of finding those teachers who work as souls and as minds.

Every child should be studied in three directions. First, to ascertain the natural trend of his impulses: Are they towards physical expression, towards manual labor, in which one would include such a wide range of opportunity as that of the mechanical factory worker and the trained skill of the electrician? Is there a latent capacity for one or other of the arts, a reaction to colour and form, or a response to music and rhythm? Is the intellectual calibre one that should warrant a definitely mental training in analysis, deduction, mathematics or logic? Then perhaps as life goes on our young people will be graded into two groups: the *mystical,* under which heading one would group those with religious, artistic and the more impractical tendencies; and the *occult,* which would include the intellectual, scientific and mental types. By the time a child is seventeen the training given should have enabled him to strike his note clearly, and should have indicated the pattern into which his life impulses will most probably run. In the first fourteen years, opportunity should be given to experiment in many fields of opportunity. Pure vocational training should not be emphasised until the later years of the educational process.

The time is coming when all children will be studied in the following directions:

1. Astrologically, to determine the life tendencies and the peculiar problem of the soul.
2. Psychologically, supplementing the best of modern psychology with a knowledge of the Seven Ray types, which colours Eastern psychology (see pages 18-23).
3. Medically, with special attention to the endocrine system, plus the usual modern methods in relation to eyes, teeth and other physiological defects. The nature of the response apparatus will be carefully studied and developed.
4. Vocationally, so as to place them later in life where their gifts and capacities may find fullest expression

and enable them thus to fulfill their group obliga-
tions.

5. Spiritually. By this I mean that the apparent age of
the soul under consideration will be studied, and the
place on the ladder of evolution will be approxi-
mately noted; mystical and introspective tendencies
will be considered and their apparent lack noted.
Coordination between:

a. Brain and the response apparatus in the outer
world of phenomena,

b. Brain and desire impulses, plus emotional reactions,

c. Brain and mind and the world of thought,

d. Brain, mind and soul,

will be carefully investigated so as to bring the entire
equipment of the child, latent or developed, into
functioning activity and to unify it into a whole.

The third question asks:

"What is the process of the unfoldment of the intellect
in man? How does the higher mind manifest, if at all, in
the growing years?"

It is not possible in the short time at our command to
deal here with the history of the progress of mental development. A study of its racial growth will reveal much, for
every child is an epitome of the whole. A study, for instance, of the growth of the God-idea in the human consciousness would prove a profitable illustration of the
phenomena of thought development. A sequence of growth
might most inadequately and briefly be tabulated as follows,
based upon the process of unfoldment in a human being:

1. Response to impact, the infant's sense awakened.
He begins to hear and see.

2. Response to possession and to acquisitiveness. The
child begins to appropriate, becomes self-conscious
and grasps for the personal self.

3. Response to the instinct governing the animal and desire nature, and to human tendencies.
4. Response to the group. The child becomes aware of his environment and that he is an integral part of a whole.
5. Response to knowledge. This begins with the impartation of informative facts, and so to the registration, through the memory, of these facts; thus are developed interest, correlation, synthesis and application to the exigencies of the life.
6. Response to the innate need to *search*. This leads to *experiment* on the physical plane, to *introspection* on the emotional plane, and to *intellectual study* and a love of reading or of listening, thus bringing the mind into some condition of activity.
7. Response to economic and sex pressure or to the law of survival. This forces him to use his equipment and knowledge and so take his place as a factor in the group life, and to promote group welfare by some aspect of active work and by the perpetuation of the species.
8. Response to pure intellectual awareness. This leads to a conscious free use of the mind, to individual thinking, to the creation of thoughtforms, and eventually to the steady orientation of the mind to a wider and wider field of realisation and awareness. These expansions of consciousness finally bring a new factor into the field of experience.
9. Response to the Thinker or the soul. With the registration of this response, the man enters into his kingdom. The above and the below become as one. The objective and the subjective worlds are unified. Soul and its mechanism function as a unit.

Towards this consummation all education should tend. Practically speaking, except in rare and highly evolved souls, the higher mind does not manifest in children, any more than it did in infant humanity. It can only truly make its presence felt when soul and mind and brain are aligned and coordinated. Flashes of insight and vision when seen in the young, are frequently the reaction of their very sensitive response apparatus to group ideas and the dominant thoughts of their time and age, or of someone in their environment.

Let me now deal briefly with the points raised concerning the attitude of the teacher, particularly towards adult aspirants.

The true teacher must deal in truth and in sincerity with all seekers. His time (in so far as he is held by the time equation on the physical plane) is too valuable to waste in social politeness or in refraining from making critical comment where a good purpose would be served. He must depend thoroughly upon the sincerity of those whom he teaches. Nevertheless, criticism and the pointing out of faults and errors does not always prove helpful; it may but increase responsibility, evoke antagonism or unbelief, or produce depression—three of the most undesirable results of the use of the critical faculty.

By stimulating their interest, by producing a subjective synthesis in the group he is teaching, and by fanning the flame of their spiritual aspiration, the group may arrive at a right discrimination as to their joint quality and necessities, and thus they will render the ordinary faultfinding attitude of the teacher unnecessary.

Those upon the teaching ray will learn to teach by teaching. There is no surer method, provided it is accompanied by a deep love, personal yet at the same time impersonal, for those who are to be taught. Above everything else, I would enjoin upon you the inculcation of the group spirit, for that is the first expression of true love. Two points only would I make:

First of all, in teaching children up to fourteen years of age, it is necessary to bear in mind that they are emotionally focussed. They need to *feel,* and rightly to feel beauty, strength and wisdom. They must not be expected to rationalise before that time, even if they show evidence of the power so to do. After fourteen years and during adolescence their mental response to truth should be drawn out and counted upon to deal with presented problems. Even if it is not there, an effort should be made to evoke it.

Secondly, an attempt should be made to approximate the child's place upon the ladder of evolution by a study of his background, his physical equipment, the nature of his response apparatus with its varied reactions, and his major interests. This enquiry sets up a subjective rapport with the child which is far more potent in its results than would be months and months of strenuously used words in the effort to convey an idea.

THEORY, METHODS AND GOALS

All that I have to say here is still in the nature of introductory remarks. Please bear this in mind. I am anxious, however, to lay a sound foundation for our future discussions on the building of the antahkarana, so that we can work intelligently, but not critically. It is essential that as we start our work it should be based on that which is today in existence. *Nature* works without any gaps, and this is so even when (from the standpoint of academic science) there is an apparent hiatus between facts and known species. In transitional periods some of the bridging forms have disappeared and the gap appears to be there. But it is not so in fact. We have not yet discovered all that is to be found in the world of phenomenal appearances. We are passing through one of the great natural transitional periods at this time. We are laying the foundation for the emergence of a new species of human being—a more highly evolved unit within the human family—hence much of our problem, and much of the present failure to meet the demands of the race, and to measure up to human need for development.

We have, in the world, a general theory as to education, and certain basic methods are universally employed. Countries vary greatly in the application of methods, and systems differ very considerably. All, however, teach these same fundamental things; they teach the youth of the country to read and write and to attain a fair measure of ability to deal with figures through instruction in elementary arithmetic. These three are curiously symbolic of the whole evolutionary unfoldment of the race.

Reading has to do with the clothing of ideas with form and is related to the first step in the creative process, wherein Deity, governed and impelled by *an idea* (embodying God's purpose and plan), converted that idea into the desired substance and clothed it with the needed outer appearance. Writing symbolises the method whereby the process is carried on, but it is of course far more personal in its implications. Reading is concerned essentially with the realisation of a clothed idea of some kind, whereas writing is, curiously enough, concerned with the individual's conscious self-relation to ideas, and his use of words in writing is the measure of the grasp he may have of these universal ideas. Arithmetic (and the power to add, to subtract, and to multiply) is related also to the creative process and concerns the production of those forms upon the physical plane which will adequately produce the idea and bring it to manifestation.

Vision might be regarded as concerning itself with the higher levels of the mental plane, whereon the idea is sensed and seen. Writing has a more definite relation to the concrete levels of the mental plane and to the ability of the man to bring through and express these visioned ideas in his own particular form. Arithmetic has a definite relation to subsequent aspects of the process and to the emergence of the idea into some correlated form upon the physical plane. The visioning of the thoughtform is a process which must be succeeded by the appropriation of as much energy by the idea as is needed to make it effective or "apparent" (esoterically speaking). Of this the symbolism of arithmetic is the expression.

From another angle, man reads his destiny in the heavens and writes out that destiny in his life upon the earth; he reduces, knowingly or unknowingly, the idea of his soul to due and proper form, so that each life adds, subtracts and multiplies, until the sum of each soul's experiencing is complete. Thus, symbolically, the three basic ideas are held in elementary education, though their true meaning is divorced from reality and the right significance is entirely lost. All that we have, however, emerging slowly and definitely through the medium of world education, is built upon this unrealised scaffolding. The fundamental necessity which today confronts the educational world is the need to relate the process of unfolding the human mentality to the world of *meaning,* and not to the world of objective phenomena. Until the aim of education is to orient a man to this inner world of realities, we shall have the misplaced emphasis of the present time. Until we can arrive in our educational objectives at the bridging of the gap between the three lower aspects of man and the soul (a bridging which must take place upon the mental levels of consciousness), we shall make but little progress in right directions and all interim activity will be inadequate to the modern need. Until the fact of the higher mind is recognised, and the place which the lower concrete mind should fill as the servant of the higher is likewise recognised, we shall have the overdevelopment of the concrete materialising faculty— with its aptitude to memorise, to correlate facts and to produce that which will meet man's lower desire—but we shall not have a humanity which can truly think. As yet, the mind reflects the lower desire nature and does not attempt to cognise the higher.

When the right method of training is instituted, the mind will be developed into a reflector or agent of the soul and so sensitised to the world of true values that the lower nature—emotional, mental and physical or vital—will become simply the automatic servant of the soul. The soul will then function on earth through the medium of the mind, thereby controlling its instrument, the lower mind. Yet at the same time, the mind will remain the recorder and reflector of all information coming to it from the world of the senses, from the emotional body, and will register also the thoughts and the ideas current in its environment. At present, it is alas true, the trained mind is regarded as the highest expression of which humanity is capable; it is viewed entirely as a personality, and the possibility of there being something which can use the mind, as the mind in its turn uses the physical brain, is overlooked.

One of the things which we shall seek to do in our studies together is to grasp the relation of the world of meaning to the world of expression; we shall attempt to study the technique whereby this world of quality (which expresses itself through the world of meaning) can be entered and understood by the integrated consciousness of the intelligent human being.

Certain words will recur again and again as we work and study together; such words as *meaning, quality, value*— all of which stand revealed in their vital spiritual significance when man learns to grasp the *fact* of the higher realities and bridges the gap between his higher and his lower consciousness. The significance also of creative activity and the right understanding of what we call genius will likewise be made clearer, and in this way creative work will no longer be regarded as unique and manifesting sporadically as is now the case but will become the subject of trained attention, and so assume its normal place in man's unfoldment. It might be added here that creative activity in the field of art becomes possible when the first aspect of the bridging energy of man can function and the soul (manifesting its third or lowest aspect) can begin to work. Creative work can be carried forward when two of the "knowledge petals" of the egoic lotus are unfolded. The man can produce, through knowledge and creative energy, something upon the physical plane which will be expressive of the soul's creative power. When two of the "love petals" are also unfolded, then a genius makes his appearance. This is a technical piece of information for those students who are studying the science of the Ageless Wisdom, but it is of no value to those who do not recognise symbology, or the fact of the higher ego or soul.

It might be of value here if I clarified my use of the words "higher ego." As you know, if you have read *A Treatise on the Seven Rays*, Vols. I and II (Esoteric Psychology), the soul is an aspect of the divine energy in time and space. We are told that the Solar Logos circumscribed for His use and for the meeting of His desire, a certain measure of the substance of space and informed it with His life and consciousness. He did this for His good purposes and in conformity with His self-realised plan and intent. Thus He submitted Himself to limitation. The human monad followed the same procedure and—in time and space—limited itself in a similar manner. On the physical plane and in the physical body, this phenomenal and transient entity controls its phenomenal appearance through the two aspects of *life* and *consciousness*. The life principle—the flow of divine energy through all forms— is temporarily seated in the heart, while the consciousness principle, the soul of all things, is located (temporarily as far as the form nature of a particular human unit is concerned) within the brain. As again you know, the life principle controls the mechanism through the medium of the blood stream, for "the blood is the life," and uses the heart as its central organ; whilst the consciousness principle uses the nervous system as its instrument, with the intricate extensions of the organ of sensitivity, the spinal column.

The objective of education should therefore be the training of the mechanism to respond to the life of the soul. The higher Self or Soul is the sumtotal of the consciousness of the Monad, again in time and space. The lower self or soul is, for our purposes, as much of that sumtotal as any one person in any one life can use and express. This activity is dependent upon the type and quality of the body nature, the mechanism produced by soul activity in other lives, and the effect of reaction to environing conditions. The increasing of soul awareness, the deepening of the flow of consciousness, and the development of an inner continuity of awareness, plus the evocation of soul attributes and as-pects upon the physical plane through the medium of its triple mechanism, constitute the objective of all education. These aspects are, as you well know:

1. *Will or purpose.* This, through education, should be developed to the point where the manifested life is governed by conscious spiritual purpose and the life tendency is correctly oriented towards reality.

The right direction of the will should be one of the major concerns of all true educators. The will-to-good, the will-to-beauty, and the will-to-serve must be cultivated.

2. *Love-wisdom.* This is essentially the unfolding of the consciousness of the whole. We call it group consciousness. Its first development is self-conscious-ness, which is the realisation by the soul that (in the three worlds of human evolution) man is the Three in One and One in Three. He can therefore react to the associated groups of lives which constitute his own little phenomenal appearance; self-conscious-

ness is, therefore, a stage on the way to group consciousness and is the consciousness of the Immediate.

Through education, this self-consciousness must be unfolded until the man recognises that his consciousness is a
corporate part of a greater whole. He blends then with the
group interests, activities and objectives. They are eventually his and he becomes group conscious. This is love. It
leads to wisdom, which is love in manifested activity. Self-
interest becomes group interest. Such should be the major
objective of all true educational endeavour. Love of self
(self-consciousness), love of those around us (group-con-
sciousness), become eventually love of the whole (God
consciousness). Such are the steps.

3. *Active Intelligence.* This concerns the unfolding of
the creative nature of the conscious, spiritual man.
It takes place through right use of the mind, with its
power to intuit ideas, to respond to impact, to trans-
late, analyse, and to construct forms for revelation.
Thus the soul of man creates. This creative process
can be described, as far as its steps are concerned, as
follows:

a. The soul creates its physical body, its phenomenal
   appearance, its outer form.

b. The soul creates, in time and space, in line with
   its desires. Thus the secondary world of phenomenal things comes into being and our modern
   civilisation is the result of this creative activity
   of the soul's desire nature, limited by form.
   Ponder on this.

c. The soul creates through the direct agency of the
   lower mind and hence the appearance of the
   world of symbols which fill our united lives with
   interest, concepts, ideas and beauty, through the
   written word, the spoken word, and the creative

arts. These are the products of the thought of the thinkers of the race.

The right direction of this already developed tendency is the aim of all true education. The nature of ideas, the modes of intuiting them, and the laws which should govern all creative work are its goals and objectives. Thus we come to the world of attributes which supplement the activity of the three aspects, in the same way that the three major rays are enhanced and aided by the work of the four minor rays. These four attributive unfoldments in man, through the activity of the soul in manifestation, are:

4. The attribute of *harmony, produced through conflict*. This leads to release and to the eventual power to create. This is one of the attributes which education should deal with from the angle of the intuition and should hold before its exponents as personality and group objectives. It is the attribute latent in all forms and is that innate urge or dis-content which leads man to struggle and progress and evolve in order finally to make atonement and union with his soul. It is the lowest aspect of that higher spiritual and monadic triad which reflects itself in the soul. It is the consciousness of harmony and beauty which drives the human unit along the path of evolution to an eventual return to his emanating Source.

Education must work, therefore, with this dissatisfaction and interpret it to those who are taught, so that they can understand themselves and work intelligently.

5. The attribute of *concrete knowledge* whereby man is enabled to concretise his concepts and so build thoughtforms whereby he materialises his visions and his dreams and brings his ideas into being. This he does through the activity of the lower concrete mind.

The true work of education is to train the lower man in
right discrimination and true sensitivity to the vision, so
that he can build true to the purpose of his soul and produce upon the earth that which will be his contribution to
the whole. It is right here that the work of modern education has to begin. Not yet can man work with intelligence
in the world of ideas and of patterns; not yet is he sensitive
to the true spiritual values. This is the goal for the disciple,
even though the masses cannot yet function on these levels.
The first thing that must be done is to train the child in
the correct use of the discriminating faculty and in the
power of choice and of directed purpose. He must be
brought to a truer understanding of the underlying purpose
of being, and be led to work with wisdom in the field of
creative activity, which means, in the last analysis, in the
right use of the "mind stuff" (the *chitta* of Patanjali). Thus
and only thus, can he be released from the control of his
lower nature.

6. The attribute of *devotion* is the next to be considered. Devotion grows out of and is the fruit of
dissatisfaction, plus the use of the faculty of choice.
According to the depths of a man's discontent, and
of his power to see clearly, he passes from one point
of temporary satisfaction to another, each time
demonstrating his devotion to a desire, to a personality, to an ideal, and to a vision, until he finally
unifies himself with the ideal which is the highest
possible to man. This is, first of all, the soul; and
then the Oversoul or God.

Educators are therefore faced with the opportunity of dealing intelligently with the innate idealism to be found in
any child, and with the interesting task of leading the youth
of the world on from one realised goal to another. But
this they must do in the future from the angle of the ultim-

ate soul objective and not, as in the past, from the angle of a particular standard of national education. This is an important point, for it will mark the shift of attention from the nonessential to the essential.

7. Finally the attribute of *order,* and the imposition of an established rhythm through the development of innate faculty to function under directed purpose and ritual. This particular attribute of divinity is now highly developed in one aspect, so that we have today much standardisation of humanity, and the autocratic imposition of a ritualistic rhythm upon public life in a large number of countries. It can be seen to perfection in the life in our public schools—but it is an undesirable perfection. This is partly due to the recognition that the unit or individual is only a part of a greater whole (a recognition which is much needed) and a part of the evolutionary unfoldment of the race. Owing, however, to our faulty application of any new truth it means as yet the submergence of that unit in the group, leaving him little opportunity for the free play of the individual will, intelligence, purpose and soul technique. Educators will have to work with this principle of innate attribute and this instinct to ordered rhythm, making it more creatively constructive and so providing, through it, a field for the unfoldment of soul powers.

I have digressed thus far so as to instill certain of the basic ideas which should underlie the educational tendencies. These thoughts, coupled with those already given, constitute a statement of the objectives before the educators of the world which you would find it of value to consider. Earlier I suggested the goal. I now link that goal up with possibilities, for I have here touched upon the equipment (aspects and attributes) which is found, in some stage of development, in every human being. It is with these hidden traits and instincts that the future educational systems must work. They must not work, as they do today, with the brain apparatus and with the lowest aspects of the mind; nor must they lay their emphasis upon the effort to impress upon that brain and mind the facts, so-called, of the evolutionary process and of physical plane investigation.

The above remarks will serve to show you that the true educator should be working with energies in a world of energy; that these energies are tinged and qualified by distinctive divine attributes, and that each human being therefore can be regarded as an aggregate of energies, dominated by some one particular type of energy which serves to make him distinctive among his fellows, and which produces the differences among human beings. If it is true that there are seven major types of energy qualifying all forms, and that these in their turn are subdivided into forty-nine types of qualified energy, the complexity of the problem emerges clearly. If it is true that all these distinctive energies play constantly upon energy-substance (spirit-matter), producing "the myriad forms which make up the form of God" (*Bhagavad Gita, XI*), and that each child is the microcosmical representation (at some stage of development) of the Macrocosm, the magnitude of the problem becomes evident, and the extent of our demanded service will call forth to the utmost the powers which any human being can express at any given moment in time and space.

You will note that these words "in time and space" have repeatedly recurred in this instruction. Why is this? Because it must constantly be remembered that we are living in the world of illusion—an illusion which is temporary and transient and which will some day disappear, taking with it the illusion of appearance, the illusion of evolutionary unfoldment, the illusion of separativeness, and the illusion of distinctive identity—that illusion which makes us say "*I am*." The educator of the future will start his service to the child with the recognition of this ephemeral and transient misconception of the soul, and will deal primarily with the mind aspect, and not with the imposition of as much imparted organised knowledge concerning phenomenal existence as the memory of the child is capable of grasping. How can I illustrate this changed attitude to you in the simplest form? Perhaps by pointing out that, whereas today parents and guardians of the child spend much of their time in answering or evading questions posed by the awakening consciousness of the child, in time to come the situation will be reversed. Parents will ceaselessly meet the demands of the emerging intelligence of the child by always enquiring of the child, Why? Why ask this? Why is it thus?—and so throwing always the responsibility of answering the questions upon the child, yet at the same time dropping the solution of the question subtly into the child's mind.

This process will begin in the fifth year of the child's life; the seeking intelligence (which is the child itself) will always be forced by the teacher into the position of *inward* search, not outer demand for a reply which can be memorised and which rests upon the authority of the older person. If this seems to you as yet impossible, remember that the children who will or have come into incarnation, after the period of increased stimulation found between the years 1935 and 1942, will normally and naturally respond to this evocation of the mind element.

One of the major functions of those who train the infant minds of the race will be to determine, as early as possible in life, which of the seven determining energies are controlling in each case. The technique to be later applied will then be built upon this important initial decision—hence again, the growing responsibility of the educator. A child's note and quality will be early determined, and his whole planned training will grow out of this basic recognition. This is not yet possible, but will shortly be so, when the quality and nature of any individual etheric body can be scientifically discovered. This development is not as distant as might be supposed or anticipated.

It is not my intention to deal with the details of this process, nor to elaborate the methods whereby the children of the race can be trained. Our objective is to deal with the more universal and immediate necessity of bridging the gap between the different aspects of the lower self, so that an integrated personality emerges; and then of bridging the gap between the soul and the spiritual triad, so that there can be the free play of consciousness and complete identification with the *One Life,* thus leading to the loss of the sense of separateness and to the merging of the part with the Whole, with no loss of identity but with no recognition of self-identification.

Here an interesting point should be carefully noted. It holds the key to future racial unfoldment. For it the new science of psychology, which has developed so remarkably during the past thirty years, is preparing us. Students should train themselves to distinguish between the sutratma and the antahkarana, between the life thread and the thread of consciousness. One thread is the basis of immortality and the other the basis of continuity. Herein lies a fine distinction for the investigator. One thread (the sutratma) links and vivifies all forms into one functioning whole and embodies in itself the will and the purpose of the expressing entity, be it man, God or a crystal. The other thread (the antahkarana) embodies the response of the consciousness within the form to a steadily expanding range of contacts within the environing whole.

The sutratma is the direct stream of life, unbroken and immutable, which can be regarded symbolically as a direct stream of living energy flowing from the centre to the periphery, and from the source to the outer expression or the phenomenal appearance. It is the *life*. It produces the individual process and the evolutionary unfoldment of all forms. It is, therefore, the path of life, which reaches from the monad to the personality, via the soul. This is the thread soul and it is one and indivisible. It conveys the energy of life and finds its final anchor in the centre of the human heart and at some central focal point in all forms of divine expression. Naught is and naught remains but life.

The consciousness thread (antahkarana) is the result of the union of life and substance or of the basic energies which constitute the first differentiation in time and space; this produces something different, which only emerges as a third divine manifestation, after the union of the basic dualities has taken place. It is the thread which is woven as a result of the appearance of life in form upon the physical plane. Speaking again symbolically, it might be said that the sutratma works from above downward and is the precipitation of life into the outer manifestation. The antahkarana is woven, evolved, and created as the result of this primary creation, and works from below upwards, from the without to the within, from the world of exoteric phenomena into the world of subjective realities and of meaning.

This "Path of Return," by means of which the race is withdrawn from outer emphasis and begins to recognise and register those inner conscious knowledges of that which is not phenomenal, has already (through the evolutionary process) reached a point of development wherein some human beings can follow along this path from the physical consciousness to the emotional, and from the emotional to the mental. That part of the work is already accomplished in many thousands of cases and what is now required is facility and right use of this power. This thread of energy, coloured by conscious sentient response, is later coloured by the discriminating consciousness of the mind, and this produces that inner integration which makes man eventually an efficient thinking being. At first, this thread is used purely for lower selfish interests; it steadily gets stronger and more potent as time goes on, until it is a definite, clear, strong thread reaching from the outer physical life, from a point within the brain, straight through to the inner mechanism. This thread, however, is not identified with the mechanism, but with the consciousness in man. Through the means of this thread a man becomes aware of his emotional life in its many forms (note this phraseology), and through it he becomes aware of the world of thought; he learns to think and begins to function consciously on the mental plane, in which the thinkers of the race—a steadily increasing number—live and move and have their being. Increasingly he learns to tread this path of consciousness, and thereby ceases to be identified with the animal outer form and learns to identify himself with the inner qualities and attributes. He lives first the life of dreams, and then the life of thought. Then the time comes when this lower aspect of the antahkarana is completed, and the first great conscious unity is consummated. The man is an integrated, conscious, living personality. The thread of continuity between the three lower aspects of the man is established and can be used. It stretches, if such a term can be used (my intent being entirely pictorial), from the centre of the head to the mind, which is in its turn a centre of energy in the world of thought. At the same time, this antahkarana is interwoven with the thread of life or the sutratma which emerges from the heart centre. The objective of evolution in form is now relatively complete.

When this stage has been reached, the sensitive feeling-out into the environing universe still continues. Man weaves a thread which is like the thread the spider weaves so amazingly. He reaches out still further into his possible environment and then discovers an aspect of himself of which he had little dreamt in the early stages of his development. He discovers the soul and then passes through the illusion of duality. This is a necessary but not a permanent stage. It is one which characterises the aspirant of this world cycle, perhaps I should say this manvantara or world period. He seeks to merge himself with the soul, to identify himself, the conscious personality, with that overshadowing soul. It is at this point, technically speaking, that the true building of the antahkarana must be begun. It is the bridge between the personality and the soul.

The recognition of this constitutes the problem with which the modern educator is faced. It is a problem that has always existed but it has concerned the individual hitherto more than the group. Now it concerns the group, for so many of the sons of men are ready for this building. Down the ages individuals have built their individual bridges between the higher and the lower, but so successful has been the evolutionary process that today the time has come for a group understanding of this emerging technique, for a group bridging, leading to a consequent or subsequent group revelation. This provides the modern opportunity in the field of education. It indicates the responsibility of the educator and points out the necessity for a new unfoldment in educational methods. The "group aspirant" must be met and the group antahkarana must be built. This, however, when rightly understood, will not negate individual effort. That always must be met; but the group understanding will increasingly aid the individual.

COORDINATION AND INTEGRATION

Thus far we have been occupied with generalisations as to the educational processes later to be applied, with the mental apparatus which comes under definite and planned training, and which is subjectively and superconsciously influenced during the process. I am presuming that you already grasp the necessity for the building of the antahkarana and for this bridging work. It is wise also to accept the fact that we are in a position to begin the definite process of constructing the link or bridge between the various aspects of man's nature, so that instead of differentiation there will be unity, and instead of a fluid, moving attention, directed here and there into the field of material living and emotional relationships, we shall learn to control the mind and to bridge the divisions, and so can direct at will the lower attention in any desired manner. Thus all aspects of man, spiritual and natural, can be focussed where needed.

This bridging work has in part already been done. Humanity has as a whole already bridged the gap between the emotional astral nature and the physical man. As I said elsewhere:

> We might generalise in the following manner as to the stages of growth and consequent ability to become the agent of ever increasing powers, tapping the resources of dynamic energy in the three worlds:
>
> *Lower types* of humanity use the sutratma as it passes through the etheric body.
>
> *Average men* utilise almost entirely that part of the sutratma which passes through the astral plane. Their reactions are largely based on desire, and are emotional.
>
> *Intellectual men* utilise the sutratma as it passes through the lower levels of the mental plane, down through the astral to the physical in its two sections. Their activities are energised by mind and not by desire, as in the earlier cases.
>
> *Aspirants on the physical plane* use the sutratma as it passes through the two lower subplanes of the

abstract levels of the mental plane, and are beginning gradually to build the antahkarana, or
the bridge between the Triad and the Personality.
The power of the Ego can begin to make itself
felt.

Applicants for initiation and initiates up to the third
initiation use both the sutratma and the antahkarana, employing them as a unit. The power
of the Triad begins to pour through, thus ener-
gising all human activities upon the physical
plane, and vitalising in ever increasing degree
the man's thought forms. The key to the formation of the Mayavirupa is found in the right
comprehension of the process.

A Treatise on Cosmic Fire, pp. 959-960.

It should be noted here that *the bridging has to be done in
the consciousness aspect,* and concerns the continuity of
man's awareness of life in all his various aspects. The energy
which is used in connecting, in consciousness, the physical
man and the astral body is focussed in the solar plexus.
Speaking in symbolical terms, many today are carrying that
bridge forward and linking the mind with the two aspects
already linked. This thread of energy emanates from, or is
anchored in, the head. A few people are steadily linking
the soul and the mind, which in its turn is linked with
the other two aspects. The soul energy, when linked with
the other threads, has its anchor in the heart. A very few
people (the initiates of the world) having effected all the
lower syntheses, are now occupied with bringing about a
still higher union with that triple Reality which uses the
soul as its medium of expression, just as the soul in its
turn is endeavouring to use its shadow, the threefold lower
man.

These distinctions and unifications are matters of form,

symbols in speech, and are used to express events and happenings in the world of energies and forces in connection with which man is definitely implicated. It is to these unifications that we refer when the subject of initiation is under consideration.

The life thread, the silver cord or the sutratma, is, as far as man is concerned, dual in nature. The life thread proper, which is one of the two threads which constitute the antahkarana, is anchored in the heart, whilst the other thread which embodies the principle of consciousness, is anchored in the head. This you already know, but this I feel the need constantly to reiterate. In the work of the evolutionary cycle, however, man has to repeat what God has already done. He must himself create, in both the world of consciousness and of life. Like a spider, man spins connecting threads, and thus bridges and makes contact with his environment, thereby gaining experience and sustenance. The spider symbol is often used in the ancient occult books and the scriptures of India in connection with this activity of the human being. The threads which man creates are triple and with the two basic threads which have been created by the soul, constitute the five types of energy which make man a conscious human being. The triple threads created by man are anchored in the solar plexus, the head and the heart. When the astral body and the mind nature are beginning to function as a unit, and the soul also is consciously connected (do not forget that it is always unconsciously linked), an extension of this fivefold thread —the basic two and the human three—is carried to the throat centre; when that occurs man can become a conscious creator on the physical plane. From these major lines of energy lesser lines can radiate at will. It is upon this knowledge that all future intelligent psychic unfoldment must be based.

In the above paragraph and its implications you have a brief and inadequate statement as to the Science of the

Antahkarana. I have endeavoured to express this in terms, symbolic if you will, which will convey some general idea of the process to your minds. We can learn much through the use of the pictorial and visual imagination. Many aspirants have already established the following links of the bridging antahkarana:

1. From the physical to the vital or etheric body. This is really an extension of the life thread between the heart and the spleen.
2. From the physical and the vital, regarding them as a unity, to the astral or emotional vehicle. This thread emanates from, or is anchored in, the solar plexus, and is carried upward by means of the aspiration till it anchors itself in the love petals of the egoic lotus.
3. From the physical and astral vehicles to the mental body. One terminal is anchored in the head, and the other in the knowledge petals of the egoic lotus, being carried forward by an act of the will.

Many, too, are in process of linking the three lower aspects, which we call the personality, with the soul itself, through meditation, discipline, service and directed attention. When this has been accomplished, a definite relation is established between the sacrifice or will petals of the egoic lotus and the head and heart centres, thus producing a synthesis between consciousness, the soul and the life principle. The process of establishing this interlinking and interrelation, and the strengthening of the bridge thus constructed, goes on until the third initiation. The lines of force are then so interrelated that the soul and its mechanism of expression are a unity. A higher blending and fusing can then go on.

It is necessary for me to stop at this point and indicate that all the above are simply word pictures of a process of energy interrelations, and have a definite value if they can introduce and make real to you the fact of the indicated processes. Some aspirants and students have the mystical consciousness highly developed, and are therefore apt to resent and regard as unnecessary the more technical and intellectual presentation of a truth which they sense and know, but which remains a truth yet undefined. It is my purpose to assist you towards a greater definiteness of realisation and expression; this should in no way detract from the wonder and the beauty of what you sense, but should increase your power to know and also to make available to others the knowledge which you have gained. In the past the mystic expressed his realisation through love and practical kindness, expressing it on the physical plane through charitable deeds and self-sacrifice, and on emotional levels by his aspiration, his vision, and his ability to express the love of God to the world. The mystic today continues with the same process, but under the evolutionary urge becomes capable of more than this. He should be able to formulate his knowledge intelligently and to express his awareness clearly, in order that he may share it with the public which is steadily growing in intelligence, but greatly needs the vision. I therefore beg of you not to resent the technical formulation of truth, for if education means anything at all, and if we are to consider the ways in which education is to be applied to bring about this bridging and synthesis, it is essential that we avoid that mental laziness and mystical inertia which are characteristic of so many mystics and the line of least resistance for many would-be disciples.

It is necessary therefore that we grasp the facts that:

1. The new education will primarily be concerned with the scientific and conscious bridging between the various aspects of the human being, thus producing coordination and synthesis and an increased

expansion of consciousness through the establishing of right lines of energy.

2. The task of the new education is therefore the co-ordination of the personality, eventually bringing about its at-one-ment with the soul.

3. The new education will deal with, analyse and interpret the laws of thought, because the mind will be regarded as the link between the soul and the brain. These laws are the means whereby:

a. Ideas are intuited.

b. Ideals are promulgated.

c. Mental concepts or thoughtforms are constructed which in due time will make their impact telepathically upon the minds of men.

4. The new education will organise and develop the lower concrete mind.

5. It will teach the human being to think from universals to particulars, as well as to undertake the analysis of particulars. There will consequently be less emphasis in future schools upon the training of the memory. Interest will greatly aid the will to recall.

6. The new education will make a man a good citizen by developing the rational aspects of his consciousness and life, teaching him to use his inherited, acquired and endowed equipment for the evidencing of the social consciousness and attitudes.

7. Above all else, the educators in the new age will endeavour to teach man the science of unifying the three aspects of himself which are covered by the general title of mental aspects:

a. The lower concrete mind.

b. The Son of Mind, the Soul, the Self.

c. The higher, abstract or intuitional mind.

or:

a. The receptive mind or common-sense.

    b. The individualised mind.

    c. The illuminating mind.

8. The educators in the new age will deal with the processes or methods to be employed in bridging the gaps in consciousness between the different aspects. Thus the Science of the Antahkarana will be brought definitely to the attention of the public.

9. The extension of this concept of bridging will be developed to include not only the internal history of man, but also the bridging between him and his fellowmen on all levels.

10. It will include also the training of the human mechanism to respond to life impacts, and to the soul. This soul is essentially intelligence, vitally used on each plane. It functions as the discriminating mind on the mental plane, as the sensitive consciousness on the emotional plane, and as the active participator in physical life. This intelligent activity is always used from the wisdom angle.

11. The new education will take into consideration:

    a. The mind and its relation to the energy body, the etheric body, which underlies the nervous system and which galvanises the physical body into activity.

    b. The mind and its relation to the brain.

    c. The mind and its relation to the seven centres of force in the etheric body, and their externalisation and utilisation through the medium of the major nerve plexi to be found in the human body, and their relation (which will become increasingly obvious) to the endocrine glands.

    d. The brain as the coordinating factor in the dense body, and its capacity to direct the activities of the man through the medium of the nervous system.

In the above statements you will see how large is our theme, and yet it is one which I intend to cover with the utmost brevity, writing only a fundamental textbook which will serve as a signpost for the production of the new culture which will distinguish the Aquarian Age. Other disciples will later elaborate my theme, but the subject is as yet so little understood that much that could be said would be meaningless, even to the most intelligent.

Modern education is beginning to give some attention to the nature of the mind and to the laws of thought. In this connection we owe much to psychology and philosophy. There is also an increasing interest in the Science of Endocrinology as a material means of producing changes, usually in deficient children and morons. Nevertheless, until modern educators begin to admit the possibility that there are central units in man which underlie the tangible and visible mechanism, and will also admit the possibility of a central powerhouse of energy behind the mind, progress in education will be relatively at a standstill; the child will not receive the initial training and the foundational ideas which will enable him to become a self-directed, intelligent human being. Psychology, with its emphasis upon the three aspects of man—thought, emotional feeling, and the bodily organism—has already made a vital contribution and is doing much to bring about radical changes in our educational systems. Much remains to be done. The interpretation of men in terms of energy and the grasping of the seven types of energy which determine a man and his activities, will bring about immediate changes.

CHAPTER II

The Cultural Unfoldment of the Race

CIVILISATION AND CULTURE

MUCH EMPHASIS is being laid today upon education—coordinating, relational, psychological, vocational and equipping. To this must be added the old method of memory training and the attempt either to infuse religion into the mind of the child or to omit it with decision and with purpose. Modern education has been primarily competitive, nationalistic and, therefore, separative. It has trained the child to regard the material values as of major importance, to believe that his particular nation is also of major importance and that every other nation is secondary; it has fed pride and fostered the belief that he, his group and his nation are infinitely superior to other people and peoples. He is taught consequently to be a one-sided person with his world values wrongly adjusted and his attitudes to life distinguished by bias and prejudice. The rudiments of the arts are taught him in order to enable him to function with the needed efficiency in a competitive setting and in his particular vocational environment. To read, to write and to be able to add and do elementary arithmetic are regarded as the minimum requirement; to know something of past events—historical, geographical, literary, philosophical and scientific—are likewise added in many countries and for certain classes of people. Some of the literature of the world is also brought to his attention.

The general level of world information is high but usually biassed, influenced either by national or religious prejudices, serving thus to make a man a citizen of his own country but not a human being with world relations. World citizenship is not emphasised. The teaching imparted stimulates the latent mass consciousness of the child, and evokes the memory (racial and individual) through the impartation of facts—uncorrelated facts—most of them unrelated to daily living. These facts could serve (if used as seed thoughts in meditation and technically employed) to recover from that race consciousness and racial memory, not only national history but past history as well. I mention this in order to emphasise the danger of such undue emphasis upon the past, for if this were done on a large scale it would prove disastrous; it would put a premium on racial and national ideals and objectives and would lead rapidly to racial crystallisation and senility—metaphorically speaking. An example of an effort in this direction was seen going on in Germany, and in a lesser way in Italy; it culminated in the Axis. Fortunately, the tide of life in the youth of any nation can be trusted to swing the thought of the race into a better direction than the evocation of past glory, so-called, and the emphasising of the things which should be left behind.

I would like here to enlarge somewhat upon the interpretation of the much used words (frequently also misused) : culture and civilisation. For it is the production of some form of culture—material or spiritual, or material and spiritual—which is the objective of all education. Education is the major agent in the world.

Civilisation is the reaction of humanity to the purpose of any particular world period. In each age, some idea must be expressed in the current racial idealism. In Atlantean times, the idea that predominated was basically sensory religious idealism or mysticism, expressing itself in terms of approach to a felt but unseen deity, an expression of the way of feeling. Yet there were highly sensitive races, composed of nations and groups who laboured over the development of the feeling nature, consciously sometimes, but mostly unconsciously. Their attitude to each other, as individuals or nations, was primarily sensitive and emotional—a state of consciousness (I cannot say state of mind) most difficult for the modern Aryan race to grasp, or even intuit, for with us the mind is beginning to function. Their attitude to the deity was equally sensitive, and their religious activities were mystical and devotional, devoid of any mental understanding. They were significantly emotional in reactions to beauty, to the terror evoked by divinity and to the emotional characteristics of God, to the sense of light and to wonder. The mysterious, the sense of awe, the following blindly of some recognised "sensitive" of a higher order than the ordinary human being, and the interpretation of God and nature in terms of feeling-perception—these laid the basis of that ancient civilisation and have largely coloured our present racial attitudes, at least up until the advent of Christ, Who wrought great changes in the human consciousness and ushered in a new civilisation. Children are still largely Atlantean in their consciousness; it is with them a form of recapitulation, analogous to the prenatal stage; the same recapitulation goes forward upon the Path when a man develops the mystical consciousness anew, after he has evoked his mental nature and prior to unfolding true occult awareness or knowledge and the reactions of the higher mind. The problem before Education is to take the Atlantean consciousness of the child and make it Aryan or mental. The Atlanteans had no educational system as we understand the term. The kings and priests intuited; the masses obeyed.

In the present race a different civilised attitude is emerging and is nearing its consummation. In each age, some idea functions and expresses itself in both racial and national idealisms. Its basic trend down the centuries has produced our modern world and this has been strictly materialistic. A nation today is regarded as civilised when it is awakened to mental values and at the same time it is demanding material values; and when the mind (the lower mind) —in its memory aspect, its discriminating and separative aspects, its analysing functions, and its ability to formulate concrete ideas based on material perception, material desire and material purposes—is receiving the training which will make a material civilisation, and has made our material civilisation what it is today. With the emphasis shifting away from feeling-perception to mental attitudes towards life, with the desire to make the material life of the citizen of every nation the dominant factor in the national thought, with the mind unfoldment consecrated to material living, and with science definitely committed to the enunciation only of the provable and concerned only with the energies of material effect, is it any wonder that the major consideration of our modern civilisation lies in the field of the economic life? We are occupied with material conditions, with the object of increasing possessions, with bettering worldly situations, elaborating physical plane living, and substituting the tangible for the intangible, the concrete for the spiritual, and physical values for the subjective values. However, these latter must some day emerge into expression.

The above statement is superficial and of so general a character that it does not deal with the relatively small minority who do sense these larger values and are working to bring about their emergence into the racial life. These people are the custodians for the advance ideals of the current civilisation, but the energy which they release works out frequently in the establishment, temporarily, of the more concrete values. My remarks are only partial, and the facts equally so. I exaggerate perhaps; yet maybe I do not. Nevertheless, the fact remains that the two great civilisations about which we can really know anything—the Aryan

and the Atlantean—present two extreme objectives or posi-
tions towards which the humanity of the two periods
directed and still direct their attention.

The Atlantean civilisation was definitely religious in its
attitudes; religion was the commonplace of life and the
raison d'être of all that was. The world after death was the
subject of interest and unwavering, unquestioning belief.
The subtle influences emanating from the unseen realms,
the forces of nature and man's relation to them through a
keen sensitivity, and the entire gamut of his emotional
attitudes constituted the life of the race, and coloured all
that there was or might have been of embryo thought. The
result of all this, inherited by us when history as we now
have it arose (from the time of the flood, whenever that
might have been), can be expressed by such words as anim-
ism, spiritualism, lower psychism and feeling. The sense
of God, the sense of immortality, the sense of subtler inner
relationships, the sense of worship and the undue sensitivity of modern man is our outstanding heritage from
the civilisations which existed upon old Atlantis.

Upon all this basic structure the exact opposite is being
imposed today, and in the reaction—normal, right and
developing—man is laying a superstructure in which the
emphasis is increasingly upon the tangible, the material,
the seen, and upon that which can be proved, diagnosed,
analysed, and utilised for the improving of man's outer
life and his material position upon the planet. Both civilisations have gone too far, and in the swing of the pendulum
we shall inevitably return to a middle position, to the "noble
middle path." This middle way, utilising the best and the
highest ideals which the two preceding civilisations have
produced, will characterise the coming Aquarian Age and
its civilisations. Such an expression of the material and
the immaterial, of the seen and the unseen, of the tangible
and the spiritual has ever been the goal and the objective
of those who comprehend the true meaning of culture. In

the last analysis, and for the purposes of our theme, civilisation concerns the masses and the racial consciousness, while culture concerns the individual and the unseen spiritual man. Therefore a civilisation which is a full expression of true culture lies far ahead in the development of the race.

Culture is the approximation of the two ways—feeling and mind; of two worlds—sensitivity and thought; and of the attitudes, relational in nature, which will enable a man to live as an intelligent, subjective being in a tangible physical world. The man of culture relates the world of meaning to the world of appearances and regards them in his mind (thus recognising them with his brain, an indication of an established link or relationship) as constituting one world with two aspects. He moves with equal freedom in both worlds, and with simultaneity as far as his consciousness or his sense of awareness is concerned. Even in Atlantean times there were those who comprehended the significance of culture as an outgrowth of civilisation.

The masses must be civilised as a step towards giving them that culture which will make of them true and significant human beings. A human being has perforce to be a man, capable of living in the world of external realities, and at the same time capable of recognising himself as living in an inner world, as a mind and a soul. He then expresses an inner subjective life of such potency that it controls and dominates the physical plane life, motivating it and giving it true direction. This attitude of the human being and the task of bringing this condition of consciousness to fruition, have been regarded for centuries as the task of organised religion, whereas it is essentially and necessarily that of education. It is true that the Church in ancient days was the educator of the time, but the emphasis was laid upon the inner and subjective life, and as a rule no attempt was made to fuse and blend the two—outer material well-being and inner spiritual existence. Education is the task of the outstanding thinkers of the race and the responsibility of all governments, one however that they seldom recognise.

Finally, we shall seek to see what are the basic ideas (beginning with the recognised instincts) which have led man, step by step, to his present struggle for world betterment, group elevation and natural self-determination with a view—unconscious for the most part—of providing a better organ of expression within the living organism, humanity.

It is therefore a platitude and truism to state that humanity is today passing through a crisis of immense proportions. The causes of this crisis must be sought in many factors. They lie in the past, in the growth through evolution of certain basic tendencies in man; in past mistakes, present opportunities and the powerful activity of the Hierarchy of Love.* The future is of great promise, provided man can learn the lessons of the present which have been clearly presented to him; he must accept them and understand clearly the nature of his problem and of the crisis with its many ramifications and various implications.

The seething turmoil in which the masses of the people are now living and the emergence of one or two key people in every nation have a close relationship. These key people make their voices heard and evoke attention; their ideas are followed—rightly or wrongly—with attention, appreciation or distrust.

The slow and careful formation of the New Group of World Servers is indicative of the crisis. They are overseeing or ushering in the New Age and are present at the birth pangs of the new civilisation and the coming into manifestation of a new race, a new culture and a new world outlook. The work is necessarily slow and those of you who are immersed in the problems and pains find it hard to view

_____

* One of the three major centres through which Deity manifests: Shamballa, where the Will of God is known; Hierarchy, where the Love of God holds sway; Humanity, embodying the Intelligence aspect of God.

the future with assurance or to interpret the present with clarity.

In the field of education united action is essential. Surely a basic unity of objectives should govern the educational systems of the nations, even though uniformity of method and of techniques may not be possible. Differences of language, of background and of culture will and should always exist; they constitute the beautiful tapestry of human living down the ages. But much that has hitherto militated against right human relations must and should be eliminated.

In the teaching of history, for instance, are we to revert to the bad old ways wherein each nation glorifies itself at the expense frequently of other nations, in which facts are systematically garbled, in which the pivotal points in history are the various wars down the ages—a history, therefore, of aggression, of the rise of a material and selfish civilisation and one which had the nationalistic and, therefore, separative spirit, which has fostered racial hatred and stimulated national prides? The first historical date usually remembered by the average British child is "William, the Conqueror, 1066." The American child remembers the landing of the Pilgrim Fathers and the gradual taking of the country from its rightful inhabitants, and perhaps the Boston Tea Party. The heroes of history are all warriors—Alexander the Great, Julius Caesar, Attila the Hun, Richard Coeur de Lion, Napoleon, George Washington and many others. Geography is largely history in another form but presented in a similar manner—a history of discovery, investigation and seizure, followed frequently by wicked and cruel treatment of the inhabitants of the discovered lands. Greed, ambition, cruelty and pride are the keynotes of our teaching of history and geography.

These wars, aggression and thefts which have distinguished every great nation without exception are facts and cannot be denied. Surely, however, the lessons of the evils which they wrought (culminating in the war 1914-1945) can be pointed out and the ancient causes of present day prejudices and dislikes can be shown and their futility emphasised. Is it not possible to build our theory of history upon the great and good ideas which have conditioned the nations and made them what they are, and emphasise the creativity which has distinguished all of them? Can we not present more effectively the great cultural epochs which—suddenly appearing in some one nation—enriched the entire world and gave to humanity its literature, its art and its vision?

The war produced great migrations. Armies marched and fought in every part of the world; persecuted peoples escaped from one land to another; welfare workers went from country to country, serving the soldiers, salvaging the sick, feeding the hungry and studying conditions. The world today is very, very small and men are discovering (sometimes for the first time in their lives) that humanity is one and that all men, no matter what the colour of their skin or the country in which they live, resemble each other. We are all intermingled today. The United States is composed of people from every known country; over fifty different races or nations compose the U.S.S.R. The United Kingdom is a Commonwealth of Nations, independent nations bound together into one group. India is composed of a multiplicity of peoples, religions and tongues—hence her problem. The world itself is a great fusing pot, out of which the One Humanity is emerging. This necessitates a drastic change in our methods of presenting history and geography. Science has always been universal. Great art and literature have always belonged to the world. It is upon these facts that the education to be given to the children of the world must be built—upon our similarities, our creative achievements, our spiritual idealisms, and our points of contact. Unless this is done, the wounds of the nations will never be healed and the barriers which have existed for centuries will never be removed.

The educators who face the present world opportunity

should see to it that a sound foundation is laid for the coming civilisation; they must undertake that it is general and universal in its scope, truthful in its presentation and constructive in its approach. What initial steps the educators of the different countries take will inevitably determine the nature of the coming civilisation. They must prepare for a renaissance of all the arts and for a new and free flow of the creative spirit in man. They must lay an emphatic importance upon those great moments in human history wherein man's divinity flamed forth and indicated new ways of thinking, new modes of human planning and thus changed for all time the trend of human affairs. These moments produced the Magna Charta; they gave emphasis, through the French Revolution, to the concepts of liberty, equality and fraternity; they formulated the American Bill of Rights and on the high seas in our own time they gave us the Atlantic Charter and the Four Freedoms. These are the great concepts which must govern the new age with its nascent civilisation and its future culture. If the children of today are taught the significance of these five great declarations and are, at the same time, taught the futility of hate and war, there is hope of a better and happier as well as of a safer world.

Two major ideas should be taught to the children of every country. They are: *the value of the individual and the fact of the one humanity.* The war boys and girls have learnt, from appearances, that human life has small value; the fascist countries have taught that the individual is of no value except in so far as he implements the designs of some dictator—a Mussolini or a Hitler. In other countries, some people and some groups—through hereditary position or financial assets—are regarded as of importance and the rest of the nation as of little importance. In still other countries, the individual regards himself of so much importance and his right to please himself of so much moment that his relation to the whole is entirely lost. Yet the value of the individual and the existence of that whole we call *Humanity* are most closely related. This needs emphasising. These two principles, when properly taught and understood, will lead to the intensive culture of the individual and then to his recognition of his responsibility as an integral part of the whole body of humanity.

In the schools of today (grammar or primary schools, high schools or secondary schools, universities or colleges, using terms in general use) there can be seen an imperfect and symbolic picture of the triple objectives of the new education: Civilisation, Culture, Unification.

The grammar or primary schools might be regarded as the custodians of civilisation; they must fit the child for citizenship, teach him his place as a social unit, and emphasise his group relations, thus fitting him for intelligent living and evoking the racial memory through the courses given, in order to lay the foundation for his human relations. Reading, writing and arithmetic, elementary history (with the emphasis upon world history), geography and poetry will be taught. They must teach him certain basic and important facts of living, foundational truths, coordination and control.

The high schools or the secondary schools should regard themselves as the custodians of culture; they should emphasise the larger values of history and literature and give some understanding of art. They should begin to train the boy or girl for that future profession or mode of life which it is obvious will *condition* them. Citizenship will be taught in larger terms and the world of true values be pointed out and idealism consciously and definitely cultivated. The practical application of ideals will be emphasised. They should teach the youth of the world in such a manner that he will begin to fuse the world of appearances and the world of values and of meaning in his consciousness. He should begin to relate the worlds of objective outer living and of inner subjective existence. I am choosing my words with care.

Our colleges and universities should be a higher extension of all that has been already done. They should beautify and complete the structure already erected and should deal more directly with the world of meaning. International problems—economic, social, political and religious—should be considered and the man or woman related still more definitely to the world as a whole. This in no way indicates neglect of individual or national problems or undertakings but it seeks to incorporate them into the whole as integral and effective parts, and thus avoid the separative attitudes which have brought about the downfall of our modern world.

The college or the university should in reality be the correspondence in the field of education to the world of the Hierarchy; it should be the custodian of those methods, techniques and systems of thought and of life which will *relate a human being to the world of souls,* to the Kingdom of God, and not only to other human beings upon the physical plane; not only to the world of phenomena but also to the inner world of values and quality.

Again I repeat, this fitting of a man for citizenship in the Kingdom of God is not essentially a religious activity, to be handled by the exponents of the great world religions. It should be the task of the higher education, giving purpose and significance to all that has been done. If this seems idealistic and impossible to you, let me assure you that by the time the Aquarian Age is in full flower, this will be the assured and recognised objective of the educators of that time.

The following sequence suggests itself as we consider the curriculum to be planned for the youth of the immediate generations:

Primary education .....Civilisation ....Ages 1-14
Secondary education ...Culture ....Ages 14-21
Higher education ......Spiritual ....Ages 21-28

It is only our economic material emphasis and pressure which force the young to work before they are mature.

It should also be remembered (and this is being more widely recognised) that the quality of the young children now coming into incarnation is steadily getting better and higher. They are in many cases abnormally intelligent, and what you (in your technical parlance) call their I.Q. is frequently phenomenally high. This will be increasingly the case, until young people of fourteen will have the equipment and intelligence of the brilliant college men and women of today.

It is not possible for me to prove the truth of these statements, but a study of the race and of the modern child in our more civilised countries will indicate trends and tendencies which may make my position sounder in your final estimation. You would all do well to study carefully this distinction between culture and civilisation.

Putting this same truth in other words, and recognising as a basic premise the essentially supernormal potentialities of the human being, we might say that:

The first effort of education to civilise the child will be to train and rightly direct his instincts.

The second obligation upon the educators will be to bring about his true culture, by training him to use his intellect rightly.

The third duty of education will be to evoke and to develop the intuition.

When these three are developed and functioning you will have a civilised, cultured and spiritually awakened human being. A man will then be instinctively correct, intellectually sound, and intuitively aware. His soul, his mind, and his brain will be functioning as they should and in right relation to each other, thus again producing co-ordination and correct alignment. Some day an analysis will be made of the contribution of the three great continents—Asia, Europe and America—to this triple unfoldment, as far as the Aryan race is concerned. The glory of humanity must, however, be remembered; it consists in this: each race has produced those who have expressed the highest which was possible in their day and time—men who blended in themselves the triplicity of instinct, intellect and intuition. Their numbers were relatively few in the early stages of mankind's unfoldment, but the process of speeding up the development is rapidly going forward, and many are today fitting themselves for the "higher education" in the true sense of the term. Much more will be accomplished when the educators of the world grasp the purpose of the process as a whole planned unfoldment, and will then give their attention to the instinctual, intellectual and intuitive training of the race in such a manner that the whole twenty-eight years of training will be seen as an ordered, directed process, and the goal will be clearly visioned.

It will be apparent, then, that those to be taught will be gauged from the angles upon which I have touched:

a. Those capable of being rightly civilised. This refers to the mass of men.

b. Those capable of being carried forward into the world of culture. This includes a very large number.

c. Those who can add to the assets of civilisation and culture "the equipment" required for the process of functioning as conscious souls, not only in the three worlds of instinctual and intellectual living, but in the world of spiritual being also, and yet with complete continuity of consciousness and with a complete triple integration.

Not all can pass into the higher grades, and this must be appreciated. The gauging of ability will be based upon an understanding of the ray types (the science of esoteric psychology), on a comprehension of the condition of the glandular and physiological equipment, upon certain specific tests, and upon the new form of astrology.

I would here make a simple request to the earnest student. Ponder on the following four statements:

1. The antahkarana expresses the quality of the magnetism which opens the door into the teaching centre of the Great White Lodge.
2. The antahkarana is the conscious integrating force.
3. The antahkarana is the medium of light transference.
4. The antahkarana concerns the continuity of man's perception.

THE PROCESS OF UNFOLDMENT

I would like to add to the preceding analogy one more, which will serve to clarify the process of unfoldment in your minds and make the entire theme (from the racial angle) still more clear and definite:

General racial development ....Civilisation ....Path of Purification
Training of the Intelligentsia .....Culture ....Path of Discipleship
Production of the Illuminati ......Illumination ...Path of Initiation

It will be apparent to you, therefore, that the whole goal of the future and of the present effort, is to bring humanity to the point where it—occultly speaking—"enters into light." The entire trend of the present urge forward, which can be noted so distinctly in the race, is to enable the race to acquire knowledge, to transmute it into wisdom by the aid of the understanding, and thus to become "fully enlightened." *Enlightenment is the major goal of education.*

It is precisely in this region of thought and of recognition that the distinction is found between the work of the Buddha and the work of the Christ. The Buddha achieved "Enlightenment" and was the first of our humanity to do so. Lesser grades of enlightenment have been frequently achieved by many previously incarnating Sons of God. Christ, because of the attainment of the Buddha and because of His own point in evolution, was enabled to inaugurate a new era and institute a new goal, wherein another divine principle was enabled to come into manifestation and to achieve general recognition. He inaugurated the "age of love" and gave to the people an expression of a new divine aspect, that of love. The Buddha culminated the "age of knowledge." The Christ began the "age of love." Both ages embody and express two major divine principles. Thus the new education has been made possible by the work of the Buddha. This will indicate to you how slowly evolution moves. The new religion has been made possible by the work and the life of the Christ. Speaking esoterically, the knowledge petals of the human egoic lotus have unfolded, and the Buddha accelerated the rapid action of this happening. Now the love petals of the egoic lotus of the human family are also unfolding— the rapidity of this occurrence being the result of Christ's action. Can you understand the significance of what I am attempting to tell you, and can you grasp the meaning of what I am going to say?

The points that I am seeking to make are as follows:

Because the three knowledge petals of the human egoic lotus are now racially unfolded (and when I use the word "racial" I mean the human family and not the Aryan race), it is now possible for the love petals to unfold. The energy flowing from the outer tier of petals has had a triple effect:

1. It has vitalised the entire body of humanity, and has produced the present speed, intelligent (or should I say "intellectual"?) civilisation, and our modern culture, wherever it is found. The *brain* of humanity is now open to vitalisation, hence mass education.

2. It has opened a channel so that the love petals can vitalise the astral body of humanity, thus leading to general cooperation and group love. The heart of humanity is now open to vitalisation, hence the philanthropic, goodwill and welfare movements of today.

3. It will make possible, eventually, the vitalising of the mind body by the will or sacrifice petals, and

this will give awareness of the Plan, directed purpose, and group synthesis.

The first of these three knowledge petals opened in Lemurian
times and brought a measure of light to the physical plane
consciousness of humanity. The second opened in Atlantean
times and brought light to the astral plane. And in our race,
the Aryan, the third petal opened and brought the light
of mental knowledge to man. Thus was completed (in the
three races) the arduous task of vitalising the threefold manifested world (physical, astral, mental), and the energy of
intelligence became a powerful, ruling factor. Now the task
of vitalising man with the energy of love is proceeding and
making much progress, and the effects (because they emanate
from the second aspect of divinity) will be produced with
great facility, and in the realm of conscious awareness. I say
this for your encouragement.

Through the activity of the energy of knowledge you
have:

Civilisation .... Culture .... Illumination

and in the second case you will have:

Cooperation .... Loving Understanding ...... Group Love

There are higher correspondences for which we have as yet
no adequate words.

Cooperative goodwill is all that can, at this time, be expected from the masses, and this is the sublimation of the
forces released through civilisation. *Loving understanding*
should be the hallmark of the cultured, wiser group, plus
an ability to correlate the world of meaning with the world
of outer effects. Ponder on this sentence. *Group love* is, and
must be, the outstanding characteristic of the Illuminati of
the world, and it is at this time the motivating power of the
Masters of the Wisdom, until such time that enough disciples
are expressive of this particular force.

When the will or sacrifice petals of the human egoic lotus are opened, there will then be the appearance of a still higher triad of correspondences. These will be known as:

Participation ....Purpose ....Precipitation

Therefore, as a result of the evolutionary processes in humanity, there will appear the following category of forces or energies, each of them demonstrating certain definite qualities, and they will parallel the opening of the petals in the human lotus (Page 56).

You can note from the tabulation that the love petals are indeed showing signs of opening and this will make clear to you the possibility of certain hoped-for events. The world has to move forward regularly and in order. Premature happenings are usually disastrous.

All this concerns the cultural unfoldment of the race and is proceeding apace. When the conditioning factors are better understood and their method and purpose are grasped, we shall see an effort on the part of those interested in education to move with greater rapidity; this will hasten the achievement of culture by the masses, and the attainment of illumination by the more intellectual group.

There is one point that I would like to make here. In the future, illumination will be viewed primarily from the intellectual angle and the whole subject will be approached mentally, and not so definitely (as is the case today) from the angle of religion. Illumination, mysticism and religion have gone hand in hand. One of the major contributions of the present age to the unfoldment of the race has been the growing recognition that spirituality is not to be confused with and confined to the acceptance and the following of the precepts contained in the world Scriptures; it cannot be held down to the implications given to these Scriptures by an orthodox priestly caste, nor can the trends of ancient theologies govern. God can be known by His works, and these works can be more easily appreciated through the revelations

EDUCATION AND SCIENCE

I. KNOWLEDGE .... Civilisation .... Culture .... Illumination
 PETALS   The Masses of Men .... The Intellectuals .... Spiritual Man
        Path of Purification .... Path of Discipleship .... Path of Initiation

Plus

RELIGION AND PHILOSOPHY

II. LOVE .... Cooperation .... Loving Understanding .... Group Love
 PETALS   The Intellectuals .... World Aspirants .... The Hierarchy

Plus

GOVERNMENTS AND SOCIAL ORDER

III. WILL AND .... Participation .... Purpose .... Precipitation
 SACRIFICE PETALS (in the Plan)   (Directed Will of (of the Plan by
              all Disciples)   the Hierarchy)

of science than by the hymns, prayers and sermons of the churches throughout the world. What then will be the task of the churches in the future? And what will be the major objective of the coming new religion? Primarily it will be to bring about the opening of the love petals, thus inaugurating an era of true cooperation, loving understanding and group love. This will be done by training the people and the individual in the rules of Right Approach.

The keynote of the new education is essentially right interpretation of life past and present and its relation to the future of mankind; the keynote of the new religion must and should be right approach to God, transcendent in nature and immanent in man, whilst the keynote of the new science of politics and of government will be right human relations and for both of these education must prepare the child.

Those working in these three groups must eventually proceed in the closest cooperation, and it is for this planned understanding and this intelligent activity of mankind that the new education must prepare. In the above comments, plus what I have given earlier, you have the few suggestions which I have sought to make in connection with the cultural unfoldment of the race. The true history of humanity, which is long and varied and lost in the speculative indications of the esotericists (which, when true, are seldom susceptible of proof), have brought humanity to a point in its evolution wherein the light of knowledge is definitely permeating the dark places of the earth. A mass of information is now available to those who have the ability to read and write—and the number of these is growing every day—whilst the means of transmission and of communication have practically annihilated time and brought the whole world together as a functioning unit. A very high level of educational attainment is also emerging in all civilised countries. The average citizen is in possession of a vast amount of data on every imaginable subject. Much of it is ill-digested and unusable, yet it tends to the general elevation of the mental process. The output of men's thoughts in writing and in speech, embodying that which is old, that which is new and modern, and that which is superficial and relatively worthless, is so vast today that it is impossible to register it, and the lifetime of a book is brief. To crown all, there is a definite effort to bring the resources of education within the reach of every man upon the planet. This eventually will be done, and the intended type of education will accomplish the following things, thus laying the ground for the future unfoldment of the higher and better education:

1. Make available to the average citizen what has "come to light" in the past.
2. Evoke interest in the new sciences and knowledge which are coming to light in the present.
3. Develop the memory and the power to recognise that which is presented to the mind.
4. Correlate the past with the present.
5. Train citizens in the rights and nature of possession, with the attention to the processes of enjoyment and right use of the material and intellectual gifts of life, and their relation to the group.
6. Indicate, after due study, the right vocation.
7. Teach the methods whereby the coordination of the Personality can be brought about.

All this will turn the man out into the arena of life with a certain amount of knowledge of what has been discovered in the past and what is his intellectual heritage; with a certain amount of mental activity, which can be developed and trained if the man himself so desires it and brings it about by the right handling of himself in relation to his environment; with certain mental ideals, dreams and speculations, which can be transmuted into valuable assets if the man is dowered with persistence, if his imaginative faculties have not been dulled by an unbalanced, enforced curriculum, and if he has been fortunate enough to have a wise teacher and some understanding senior friends.

It will be apparent to you also that the task of the new education is to take the civilised masses and lead them on to the point where they are cultured; to take likewise the cultured people and train them in the ways of the Illuminati. Eventually it will be found that what is now taught in the schools of the esotericists will be part of the acknowledged curriculum imposed upon the rising generation, and that the teaching given to the advanced, thinking people of the world today will be adapted to the needs of the youth of the period.

THE NATURE OF ESOTERICISM

Educators in the new age will lay an increasing emphasis upon the esoteric approach, and it might be of service if I here attempted to define esotericism in terms of the general average intelligence of esoteric students and their point in evolution. I would remind you that true esotericism is a far deeper thing (from the angle of the Hierarchy) than you can appreciate.

One of the most inadequate of the definitions of esotericism is that it concerns that which is concealed and hidden and which, even though suspected, still remains unknown. The inference is that to be an esotericist is to be among those who seek to penetrate into a certain secret realm to which the ordinary student is not permitted to penetrate. If this were all that it is, then every scientist and every mystic would represent the approach of the mental type and of the developed emotional type to the world of esotericism and of the hidden realities. This would not, however, be accurate. The mystic is never a true esotericist, for he is not dealing in his consciousness with energies and forces, but with that vague "Something other" (called God, the Christ, the Beloved) and therefore, in reality, with that which satisfies the hunger of his soul. The scientist who is now so rapidly dealing with and entering into the world of forces and energies, is in reality a true esotericist—even if, in his effort to control the sought-for energies, he denies their source. That is of relatively small moment; later he will recognise their emanating source.

The basic approach for all who endeavour to grasp esotericism, or to teach esoteric students, is to lay the emphasis upon the world of energies and to recognise that behind all happenings in the world of phenomena (and by that I mean the three worlds of human evolution) exists the world of energies; these are of the greatest diversity and complexity, but all of them move and work under the Law of Cause and Effect. It is hardly necessary for me therefore to indicate the very practical nature of this definition and its applicability to the life of the individual aspirant, to community life and world affairs, or to the immediate conditioning levels of experimental spiritual energies which are constantly seeking impact upon or contact with the world of phenomena. This they do, under spiritual direction, in order to implement the Plan. The above statement is foundational in its importance; all other definitions are implicit in it, and it is the first important truth anent esotericism which must be learnt and applied by each aspirant to the mystery and the universality of that which moves the worlds and underlies the evolutionary process.

The first task of the esotericist is to comprehend the nature of the energies which are seeking to condition him and which work out into expression on the physical plane through the medium of his equipment or his vehicle of manifestation. The esoteric student has, therefore, to grasp that:

1. He is an aggregation of forces, inherited and conditioned by what he has been, plus a great antagonistic force which is not a principle and which we call the physical body.

2. He is sensitive to and should be increasingly aware of certain energies, at present unknown and of no use to him; of these he must eventually become aware, if he is to move deeper into the world of hidden forces. They may be energies which, for him, would be evil were he to work with them, and these must be distinguished and discarded; there are others which he must learn to use, for they would prove beneficial and would increase his knowledge, and should therefore be regarded as good. Bear in mind, however, that energies per se are neither bad nor good. The Great White Lodge, our spiritual Hierarchy, and the Black Lodge employ the same universal energies but with different motives and objectives; both groups are groups of trained esotericists.

The esotericist in training has, therefore:

1. To become aware of the nature of the forces which constitute his personality equipment and which he himself magnetically brought into expression in the three worlds. They form a combination of active forces; he must learn to differentiate between strictly physical energy, which is automatic in its response to other and inner energies, and those which come from emotional and mental levels of consciousness, focussing through the etheric body which, in turn, motivates and galvanises his physical vehicle into certain activities.

2. To become sensitive to the impelling energies of the soul, emanating from the higher mental levels. These seek to control the forces of the threefold man when a certain definite point in evolution is reached.

3. To recognise the conditioning energies in his envir-

onment, seeing them not as events or circumstances
but as *energy in action;* by this means he learns to
find his way behind the scene of outer happenings
into the world of energies, seeking contact and qualifying for the bringing about of certain activities. He
thus acquires entrance into the world of meaning.
Events, circumstances, happenings and physical phenomena of every kind are simply symbols of what is
occurring in the inner worlds, and it is into these
worlds that the esotericist must enter as far as his
perception permits; he will sequentially discover
worlds which will call for his scientific penetration.

4. For the majority of aspirants, the Hierarchy itself
remains an esoteric realm which demands discovery
and which will accept penetration. I am choosing
my words with care in an effort to evoke your esoteric response.

Beyond this point of humanity's destined goal I seek not
to go; to initiates and disciples who have not yet taken the
Initiation of Transfiguration, the higher realms of awareness and the "secret Place of the Most High" (the Council
Chamber of Sanat Kumara) remain deeply esoteric. It is a
higher realm of energies—planetary, extra-planetary and
inter-planetary; with them educators have no concern and
with their consideration the teaching staff of an esoteric
school is not called upon to deal. The task is to train students in the recognition of energy and force; to discriminate
between the various types of energy, both in relation to themselves and to world affairs, and to begin to relate that which
is seen and experienced to that which is unseen, conditioning
and determining. This is the esoteric task.

There is a tendency among esoteric students, particularly
those in the older Piscean groups, to regard any interest
in the energies producing world events or which concern
governments and politics as antagonistic to esoteric and

spiritual endeavour. But the newer esotericism which the more modern groups and the more mental types will sponsor sees all events and world movements and national governments, plus all political circumstances, as expressions of the energies to be found in the inner world of esoteric research; therefore they see no sound reason for excluding such an important aspect of human affairs from their reasoning and thinking and from the discovery of those new truths and techniques which may bring about the new era of right human relations. They ask: Why omit political research from the spiritual curriculum? They deem it to be of equal if not of greater importance than the activity of the churches; governments condition people and aid in the production of any current civilisation, forcing the masses of men into certain needed lines of thought. The churches and men everywhere need to learn that there is nothing in the entire world of phenomena, of forces and of energies, which cannot be brought under the control of that which is spiritual. All that exists is, in reality, spirit in manifestation. The masses today are becoming politically-minded, and this is viewed by the Masters as a great step forward. When the spiritually-minded people of the world include this relatively new area of human thought and its international activity within the field of their esoteric research, very great progress will be made.

Let me give you one simple illustration: War is, factually, a great explosion of energies and forces, generated on the inner planes where the esotericist ought to be working (but is seldom to be found), and finding its dire and catastrophic expression upon the physical plane. This is indicated today by the constant use of the terms "Forces of Light" and "Forces of Evil." When the inner, esoteric and predisposing causes of war are discovered through esoteric research, then war and wars will come to an end. This is in the nature of truly esoteric work, but is scorned by present day esotericists who regard themselves as spiritually superior to such affairs and—in their ivory tower—concentrate on their own development, plus a little philosophy.

One point should here be stated: Esotericism is not in any way of a mystical and vague nature. It is a science—essentially the science of the soul of all things—and has its own terminology, experiments, deductions and laws. When I say "soul," I refer to the animating consciousness found throughout nature and on those levels which lie outside the territory usually called nature. Students are apt to forget that every level of awareness, from the highest to the lowest, is an aspect of the cosmic physical plane, and is therefore (from the angle of evolutionary process) material in nature, and (from the angle or point of view of certain divine Observers) definitely tangible and formed of creative substance. The esotericist is dealing with substance all the time; he is concerned with that living, vibrant substance of which the worlds are made and which—inherited as it is from a previous solar system—is coloured by past events, and is (as has been said) "already tinged with karma." It should also be noted that just as the physical plane, so familiar to us, is not regarded as a principle by the esoteric student, so the cosmic physical plane (from the standpoint of the cosmic lives) is likewise "not a principle." I give you here much food for thought.

It might be stated that the esotericist is occupied in discovering and working with those principles which energise each level of the cosmic physical plane and which are, in reality, aspects of the qualified life energy which is working in and through unprincipled substance. His task is to shift the focus of his attention away from the substance-form side of existence and to become aware of that which has been the source of form production on any specific level. It is his task to develop within himself the needed responsiveness and sensitivity to the quality of the life dominating any form until he arrives eventually at the quality of the ONE LIFE which animates the planet and within Whose activity we live and move and have our being.

To do this, he must first of all discover the nature of his own qualified energies (and here the nature of the governing rays enters in) which are expressing themselves through his three lower vehicles of manifestation, and later through his integrated personality. Having arrived at a measure of this knowledge and having oriented himself towards the qualified life aspect, he begins to develop the subtle, inner mechanism through which contact can be made with the more general and universal aspects. He learns to differentiate between the quality or karmic predispositions of the "unprincipled" substance of which his form and all forms are made, and the qualified principles which are seeking expression through those forms and, incidentally, to redeem, salvage and purify them so that the substance of the next solar system will be of a higher order than that of the present one, and consequently more responsive to the will aspect of the Logos.

Viewed from this angle, *esotericism is the science of redemption,* and of this all World Saviours are the everlasting symbol and exponents. It was to redeem substance and its forms that the planetary Logos came into manifestation, and the entire Hierarchy with its great Leader, the Christ (the present world Symbol) , might be regarded as a hierarchy of redeemers, skilled in the science of redemption. Once They have mastered this science, They can then pass on to the Science of Life and deal with the energies which will eventually hold and use the qualified, redeemed and then principled substance and forms. It is the redemption of unprincipled substance, its creative restoration and spiritual integration, which is Their goal; the fruits of Their labour will be seen in the third and final solar system. Their activity will produce a great spiritual and planetary fusion, of which the fusion of personality and soul (at a certain point upon the path of evolution) is the symbol in the microcosmic sense. You can see by this the close relation between the work of the individual aspirant or disciple as he redeems, salvages and purifies his threefold body of manifestation and the work of the planetary Logos as He performs a similar task in connection with the "three periodical vehicles" through which He works: His personality vehicle, His soul expression and His monadic aspect.

By means of all that I have said you will realise that I am endeavouring to take the vagueness out of the word "esotericism," and to indicate the extremely scientific and practical nature of the enterprise upon which all esotericists are embarked.

Esoteric study, when coupled with esoteric living, reveals in time the world of meaning and leads eventually to the world of significances. The esotericist starts by endeavouring to discover the reason *why;* he wrestles with the problem of happenings, events, crises and circumstances in order to arrive at the meaning they should hold for him; when he has ascertained the meaning of any specific problem, he uses it as an invitation to penetrate more deeply into the newly revealed world of meaning; he then learns to incorporate his little personal problems into the problem of the larger Whole, thus losing sight of the little self and discovering the larger Self. The true esoteric viewpoint is always that of the larger Whole. He finds the world of meaning spread like an intricate network over all activity and every aspect of the phenomenal world. Of this network the etheric web is the symbol and design; and the etheric web to be found between the centres up the individual spinal column is its microcosmic correspondence, like a series of doors of entrance into the larger world of meaning. This, in reality, concerns the true Science of the Centres to which I have frequently referred. They are modes of conscious entry (when developed and functioning) into a world of subjective realities and into hitherto unknown phases of the divine consciousness.

Esotericism is not, however, concerned with the centres as such, and esotericism is not an effort scientifically to awaken the centres, as many students think. Esotericism really is training in the ability to function freely in the world of meaning; it is *not* occupied with any aspect of the mechanical form; it is occupied entirely with the soul aspect—the aspect of Saviour, Redeemer and Interpreter—and with the mediating principle between life and substance. This mediating principle is the soul of the individual aspirant or disciple (if one may use such misleading wording) ; it is also the anima mundi in the world as a whole.

Esotericism therefore involves a life lived in tune with the inner subjective realities; it is only possible when the student is intelligently polarised and mentally focussed; it is only useful when the student can move among these inner realities with skill and understanding. Esotericism involves also comprehension of the relation between forces and energies and the power to use energy for the strengthening, and then for the creative use of the forces contacted; hence their redemption. Esotericism uses the forces of the third aspect (that of intelligent substance) as recipients of the energies of the two higher aspects and, in so doing, salvages substance. Esotericism is the art of "bringing down to earth" those energies which emanate from the highest sources and there "grounding them" or anchoring them. As illustration: it was an esoteric activity of a world-wide group of students which resulted in the giving out of the teaching anent the New Group of World Servers,* thereby grounding and fixing in the consciousness of humanity the fact of the existence and work of this basically subjective group; thus the work of that group was focussed and their redeeming activity intensified.

----

* *A Treatise on White Magic*, pages 398-433; *A Treatise on the Seven Rays*, Vol. II (Esoteric Psychology), pages 629-751.

All true esoteric activity produces light and illumination; it results in the inherited light of substance being intensified and qualified by the higher light of the soul—in the case of humanity consciously functioning. It is therefore possible to define esotericism and its activity in terms of light, but I refrain from doing so because of the vagueness and the mystical application hitherto developed by esotericists in past decades. If esotericists would accept, in its simplest form, the pronouncement of modern science that *substance* and *light* are synonymous terms, and would recognise also that the light which they can bring to bear on substance (the application of energy to force) is equally substantial in nature, a far more intelligent approach would be made. The esotericist *does* deal with light in its three aspects, but it is preferable today to attempt a different approach until—through development, trial and experiment—the esotericist knows these triple differentiations in a practical sense and not just theoretically and mystically. We have to live down some of the mistakes of the past.

I have given you many other definitions in my various books, and some of them were quite simple; they can carry meaning today and will come to have more abstruse significances to you later on.

I would challenge all esotericists to attempt the practical approach which I have here outlined. I would ask them to live redemptive lives, to unfold their innate mental sensitivity, and to work continuously with the meaning which is to be found behind all individual, community, national and world affairs. If this is done, then the light will suddenly and increasingly shine upon your ways. You can become light-bearers, knowing then that "in that light you will see Light"—and so will your fellowmen.

CHAPTER III

The Next Step in the Mental Development of Humanity

THE PRESENT TRANSITION PERIOD

THERE ARE three immediate steps ahead of the educational systems of the world, and some progress has already been made towards taking them. Bear in mind that under the evolutionary urge such steps are often made without any understanding of the true objectives, or any real grasp of the emerging significance and purpose. They are simply made because the need of the time makes them the obvious next step, because the old system is failing to accomplish its intended purpose, because the results are patently undesirable, and because some man of vision works out a newer method and imposes his will upon those around him in order to demonstrate the new ideal. These three immediate steps are:

First: The development of more adequate means of understanding and studying the human being. This will be made possible in three ways:

1. The growth and the development of the *Science of Psychology*. This is the science of the essential man, and is at this time being more generally recognised as useful to, and consistent with, the right development of the human unit. The various schools of psy-

chology, so numerous and separative, will each eventually contribute its particular and peculiar truth, and thus the real science of the soul will emerge from this synthesis.

2. The growth and the development of the *Science of the Seven Rays*. This science will throw light upon racial and individual types; it will clearly formulate the nature of individual and racial problems; it will indicate the forces and energies which are struggling for expression in the individual and in the race; and when the two major rays and the three minor rays (which meet in every man) are recognised and studied by the educator in connection with the individual, the result will be right individual and group training, and correct vocational indications.

3. The acceptance of the *Teaching anent the Constitution of Man* given by the esotericists, with the implied relation of soul and body, the nature of those bodies, their qualities and purpose, and the interrelation existing between the soul and the three vehicles of expression in the three worlds of human endeavour.

In order to bring this about, the best that the East has to offer and the knowledge of the West will have to be made available. The training of the physical body, the control of the emotional body, and the development of right mental apprehension must proceed sequentially, with due attention to the time factor, and also to that period wherein planned coordination of all aspects of the man should be carefully developed.

Second: The recognition of the facts of *Esoteric Astrology*.

When this becomes possible there will be an opportunity to train the child from its earliest breath. A careful record will be kept of that exact moment, the moment of birth, or of the first breath, often accompanied by the first cry. Character delineations will be noted and compared with the developing subject and also with the ray chart, and the relation of these two—the horoscope and the ray chart—will be subjected to a careful analysis every seven years. These processes will guide the educator in the necessary steps which should be taken wisely to hasten the child's unfoldment. Modern ordinary astrology, with its prevision factor, its emphasis upon the nonessential points and upon the physical concerns of the incarnated soul, will be gradually superseded by the recognition of relationships, of life objectives, of basic character predispositions and of the soul purpose, and much will then become possible to the wise friend and guide of youth—which is what every educator should aim to be.

Third: The admittance of the fact of the *Law of Rebirth* as a governing, natural process.

This will serve as a determining factor in the racial life and will bring much light into the educational field. The tracing and relating of basic trends to past racial unfoldments and to ancient racial episodes will prove of interest and of import, and though the recovery of past lives will be of no interest, the recognition of characteristics which have been inherited from the past will serve real purpose. Young people will then be studied from the standpoint of their probable point upon the ladder of evolution, and will be grouped as:

a. Lemurians, with physical predispositions.
b. Atlanteans, with emotional dominance.
c. Aryans, with mental tendencies and inclinations.
d. New race, with group qualities and consciousness and idealistic vision.

The time factor (from the angle of present attainment and possible goal in the immediate life) will be carefully consid-

ered, and in this way there will be no lost motion; the boy
or girl will meet with understanding help and with analysis,
but not with ignorance and criticism; they will be safe-
guarded and not punished; they will be stimulated and not
held back; they will be occultly *recognised,* and therefore
will not constitute a problem.

It will be obvious to you that some decades must elapse
before such a state of affairs can become possible and usual,
but you will note that I have said "decades" and not "centuries." The earlier experiments along this line will become
possible only in small schools of specially selected children or
small colleges with a picked and trained faculty, cautiously
ready to experiment. It is only by the demonstration of the
advantage of the above methods of studying and training
children that national educational authorities will be convinced of the light which these modes of approach to the deli-
cate task of fitting the human being for life, can throw upon
the problem. At the same time, it is essential that such
schools and colleges preserve as much of the ordinary demanded curriculum as is possible, so as to be able to demonstrate their adequacy when in competition with other recognised educational systems.

If a true understanding of the seven ray types, of the con-
stitution of man and of astrology, plus a right application of
a synthetic psychology is of any use at all, it must demonstrate itself in the production of a correctly coordinated,
wisely developed, highly intelligent and mentally directed
human being.

The trouble with the majority of the previous attempts
to impose a form of the new age education upon the modern
child has been of a twofold nature:

First, there has been no compromise between the present
form of education and the desired ideal; there has been no
scientific bridging done; and no attempt has been made to
correlate the best of the present methods (probably well
adapted to the child of the period) and some of the more

appropriate methods embodied in the new vision, particularly those which can be easily approximated to those in use. Only in this way can the sequential steps be taken, until the new education is an accomplished fact and the old and the new techniques are welded into one appropriate whole. The visionary idealist has hitherto held the field and thus slowed up the process.

Second, the new methods can be tried out successfully only through the medium of most carefully selected children. These children must be watched from babyhood, their parents must be willing to cooperate in the task of providing right early conditions and right atmosphere, and their lives (their case histories) must be studied along the lines suggested earlier in this instruction.

Visionary, mystical hopes and dreams are useful in so far as they indicate a possible goal; they are of small use in determining process and method. The imposition of the new age ways in education, upon a child who is basically Atlantean or early Aryan in his consciousness, is a fruitless task and will do little really to help him. It is for this reason that a careful analysis of the child must be made from the very moment of birth. Then, with as full information as possible, the educator will endeavour to meet the need of the three major types of children: The Atlantean, or basically emotional, sensuous type; the early Aryan, or emotional-mental type; the later Aryan or early New Age type, which will be predominantly mental, and at the same time idealistic, brilliant, coordinated, and a personality.

The question here arises: How can such methods be employed without the whole process appearing too much like a laboratory experiment in which the child is regarded as a specimen—or a sample child—to be subjected to certain types of impression in which he is deprived of that free scope to be himself—an individual (which seems at all times so desirable and necessary)—and in which the entire process appears as an infringement of the dignity which is the heritage of every human being? Such educational questions and objectives sound important and fine and imposing, but what do they really mean?

I have suggested that the textbooks be rewritten in terms of right human relations and not from the present nationalistic and separative angles. I have also pointed out certain basic ideas which should be immediately inculcated: the unique value of the individual, the beauty of humanity, the relation of the individual to the whole and his responsibility to fit into the general picture in a constructive manner and voluntarily; I have noted the imminence of the coming spiritual renaissance. To all of these I would like to add that one of our immediate educational objectives must be the elimination of the competitive spirit and the substitution of the co-operative consciousness. Here the question at once arises: How can one achieve this and at the same time bring about a high level of individual attainment? Is not competition a major spur to all endeavour? This has hitherto been so, but it need not be.

Today the average child is, for the first five or six years of his life, the victim of his parents' ignorance or selfishness or lack of interest. He is frequently kept quiet and out of the way because his parents are too busy with their own affairs to give him the needed time—busy with nonessential matters, compared to the important and essential business of giving their child a right start upon the pathway of life in this incarnation. He is left to his own resources or those of some ignorant nursemaid, at a stage when a destructive little animal should be developed into a constructive little citizen. He is sometimes petted and often scolded. He is dragged hither and thither, according to his parents' whims and interest, and he is sent to school with a sense of relief on their part, in order to get him occupied and out of the way. At school, he is frequently under the care of some young, ignorant though well-meaning person whose task it is to teach him the rudiments of civilisation—a certain superficial attitude and form of manners which should govern his relations to the world of men, an ability to read and write and figure, and a smattering (rudimentary indeed) of history and geography and good form in speech and writing.

By that time however the mischief is done and the form which his later educational processes may take, from the age of eleven onward, is of small moment. An orientation has been effected, an attitude (usually defensive, and therefore inhibiting) has been established, a form of behaviour has been enforced or imposed which is superficial, and which is not based upon the realities of right relationships. The true person which is found in every child—expansive, out-going and well-meaning as are the bulk of children in in-fancy—has consequently been driven within, out of sight, and has hidden itself behind an outer shell which custom and tuition have enforced. Add to this a multitude of mis-understandings on the part of loving but superficial and well-intentioned parents, a long series of small catastrophies in relation to others, and it is obvious that the majority of children get off to a wrong start and begin life basically han-dicapped. The damage done to children in the plastic and pliable years is often irremediable and is responsible for much of the pain and suffering in later life. What then can be done? What, apart from the more technical approaches out-lined by me in earlier parts of this instruction, should be the effort on the part of parents and educators?

First, and above everything else, the effort should be made to provide an atmosphere wherein certain qualities can flourish and emerge.

1. *An atmosphere of love,* wherein fear is cast out and the child realises he has no cause for timidity, shy-ness or caution, and one in which he receives cour-teous treatment at the hands of others, and is ex-pected also to render equally courteous treatment in return. This is rare indeed to find in schoolrooms

or in homes for that matter. This atmosphere of love is not an emotional, sentimental form of love but is based upon a realisation of the potentialities of the child as an individual, on a sense of true responsibility, freedom from prejudice, racial antagonisms, and above everything else, *upon compassionate tenderness.* This compassionate tenderness is founded on the recognition of the difficulty of living, upon sensitivity to the child's normally affectionate response, and upon a knowledge that love always draws forth what is best in child and man.

2. *An atmosphere of patience,* wherein the child can become, normally and naturally, a seeker after the light of knowedge; wherein he is sure of always meeting with a quick response to inquiry and a careful reply to all questions, and wherein there is never the sense of speed or hurry. Most children's natures are warped by the rush and hurry of those with whom they are perforce associated. There is no time to instruct them and to reply to their small and most necessary inquiries, and the time factor therefore becomes a menace to right development, and leads eventually to a life of evasions and of wrong perspectives. Their standard of values becomes distorted by watching those with whom they live, and much of it is brought to their attention by the impatience which is displayed towards them. This impatience on the part of those upon whom they are so pathetically dependent, sows in them the *seeds of irritation,* and more lives are ruined by irritation than can be counted.

3. *An atmosphere of ordered activity,* wherein the child can learn the first rudiments of responsibility. The children who are coming into incarnation at this time, and who can profit by the new type of education, are necessarily on the very verge of soul consciousness. One of the first indications of such soul contact is a

rapidly developing sense of responsibility. This should be carefully borne in mind, for the shouldering of small duties and the sharing of responsibility (which is always concerned with some form of group rela- tion) is a potent factor in determining a child's char- acter and future vocation.

4. *An atmosphere of understanding,* wherein a child is always sure that the *reasons* and motives for his ac- tions will be recognised, and that those who are his older associates will always comprehend the nature of his motivating impulses, even though they may not always approve of what he has done or of his activities. Many of the things which the average child does are not in themselves naughty or wicked or intentionally bad. They are frequently prompted by a thwarted inquiring spirit, by the desire to retaliate for some injustice (based on the adult's lack of un- derstanding his motivation), by an inability to employ time rightly (for the directional will is often, at this age, entirely quiescent and will not become active until the mind is beginning to function), and by the urge to attract attention—a necessary urge in the de- velopment of self-consciousness, but one which needs understanding and most careful guidance.

It is the older generation who foster in a child an early and most unnecessary sense of guilt, of sinfulness and of wrongdoing. So much emphasis is laid upon petty little things that are not really wrong but are annoying to the parent or teacher, that a true sense of wrong (which is the recognition of failure to preserve right relations with the group) gets overlaid and is not recognised for what it is. The many small and petty sins, imposed upon children by the constant reiteration of "No," by the use of the word "naughty," and based largely on parental failure to under- stand and occupy the child, are of no real moment. If these aspects of the child's life are rightly handled, then the truly wrong things, the infringements upon the rights of others, the encroachments of individual desire upon group require- ments and conditions, and the hurting or damaging of others in order to achieve personal gain, will emerge in right perspective and at the right time. Then the voice of con- science (which is the whisper of the soul) will not be dead- ened, and the child will not become anti-social. He only becomes anti-social when he has not met with understanding and therefore does not understand or when circumstances demand too much of him.

You might inquire here, after considering these four types of atmosphere regarded as essential preliminary steps to the new education: How, in this case, do you make allowance for inherited instinct, normal inclination based upon the point in evolution and character tendencies which are determined by ray forces and astrological influences?

I have not emphasised them there, even while recognis- ing them as conditioning factors which must receive atten- tion, because I have been dealing with the unnecessary and vast accumulation of imposed difficulties which are *not* in- nate in the child or truly characteristic of him, but which are the result of his environment and the failure of his home circle and existing educational agencies rightly to aid him in making his adjustments to life and his period. When there is wise handling from infancy, when the child is re- garded as the most important concern of his parents and teachers (because he is the future in embryo), and when, at the same time, he is taught a sense of proportion by right integration into the little world of which he is a part, we shall see the major lines of difficulty, the basic character trends and the gaps in his equipment emerge clearly. They will not be hidden until the years of adolescence by the little sins and evasions and by the petty embryonic com- plexes, which have been imposed upon him by others and did not form a part of his innate equipment when he came into incarnation. Then these major difficulties can be handled in an enlightened manner, and those basic tendencies which are undesirable can be offset through the wisdom of the educator, plus the cooperation and understanding of the child. *He will understand because he is understood and consequently fearless.*

Let us now formulate a more extended plan for the future education of the children of the world. We have noted that in spite of universal educational processes and many centres of learning in every country, we have not yet succeeded in giving our young people the kind of education which will enable them to live wholly and constructively. The development of world education has been progressively along three main lines, starting in the East and culminating today in the West. Naturally, I am speaking only in terms of the last two or three thousand years. In Asia, we have had the intensive training, down the centuries, of certain carefully chosen individuals and a complete neglect of the masses. Asia and Asia alone has produced those outstanding figures who are, even today, the object of universal veneration— Lao Tze, Confucius, the Buddha, Shri Krishna and the Christ. They have set Their mark upon millions and still do.

Then in Europe, we have had educational attention concentrated upon a few privileged groups, giving them a carefully planned cultural training but teaching only the necessary rudiments of learning to the masses. This produced periodically such important epochs of cultural expression as the Elizabethan period, the Renaissance, the poets and writers of the Victorian era and the poets and musicians of Germany, as well as the clusters of artists whose memory is perpetuated in the Italian School, the Dutch and the Spanish groups.

Finally, in the newer countries of the world, such as the United States, Australia and Canada, mass education was instituted and was largely copied throughout the entire civilised world. The general level of cultural attainment became much lower; the level of mass information and competency considerably higher. The question now arises: What will be the next evolutionary development in the educational world?

Let us remember one important thing. What education can do along undesirable lines has been well demonstrated in Germany with its wrecking of idealism, its inculcation of wrong human relations and attitudes and its glorification of all that is most selfish, brutal and aggressive. Germany has proved that educational processes when properly organised and supervised, systematically planned and geared to an ideology, are potent in effect, especially if the child is taken young enough and if he is shielded from all contrary teaching for a long enough time. Let us remember at the same time that this demonstrated potency can work two ways and that what has been wrought out along wrong lines can be equally successful along right ones.

We need also to realise that we must do two things: We must place the emphasis educationally upon those who are under sixteen years of age (and the younger the better) and, secondly, that we must begin with what we have, even whilst recognising the limitations of the present systems. We must strengthen those aspects which are good and desirable; we must develop the new attitudes and techniques which will fit a child for complete living and so make him truly human— a creative, constructive member of the human family. The very best of all that is past must be preserved but should only be regarded as the foundation for a better system and a wiser approach to *the goal of world citizenship*.

It might be of value at this point to define what education can be, if it is impulsed by true vision and made responsive to sensed world need and to the demands of the times.

Education is the training, intelligently given, which will enable the youth of the world to contact their environment with intelligence and sanity, and adapt themselves to the existing conditions. This today is of prime importance and is one of the signposts in a world which has fallen to pieces.

Education is a process whereby the child is equipped with the information which will enable him to act as a good citizen and perform the functions of a wise parent. It should take into consideration his inherent tendencies, his racial and national attributes, and then endeavour to add to these that knowledge which will lead him to work constructively in his particular world setting and prove himself a useful citizen. The general trend of his education will be more psychological than in the past and the information thus gained will be geared to his peculiar situation. All children have certain assets and should be taught how to use them; these they share with the whole of humanity, irrespective of race or nationality. Educators will, therefore, lay emphasis in the future upon:

1. A developing mental control of the emotional nature.
2. Vision or the capacity to see beyond what is, to what might be.
3. Inherited, factual knowledge upon which it will be possible to superimpose the wisdom of the future.
4. Capacity wisely to handle relationships and to recognise and assume responsibility.
5. The power to use the mind in two ways:
   a. As the "commonsense" (using this word in its old connotation), analysing and synthesising the information conveyed by the five senses.
   b. As a searchlight, penetrating into the world of ideas and of abstract truth.
   Knowledge comes from two directions. It is the result of the intelligent use of the five senses and it is also developed from the attempt to seize upon and understand ideas. Both of these are implemented by curiosity and investigation.

Education should be of three kinds and all three are necessary to bring humanity to a needed point of development.

It is, first of all, a process of acquiring facts—past and present—and of then learning to infer and gather from this mass of information, gradually accumulated, that which can be of practical use in any given situation. This process involves the fundamentals of our present educational systems.

It is, secondly, a process of learning wisdom as an outgrowth of knowledge and of grasping understandingly the meaning which lies behind the outer imparted facts. It is the power to apply knowledge in such a manner that sane living and an understanding point of view, plus an intelligent technique of conduct, are the natural results. This also involves training for specialised activities, based upon innate tendencies, talents or genius.

It is, finally, a process whereby unity or a sense of synthesis is cultivated. Young people in the future will be taught to think of themselves in relation to the group, to the family unit and to the nation in which their destiny has put them. They will also be taught to think in terms of world relationship and of their nation in relation to other nations. This covers training for citizenship, for parenthood, and for world understanding; it is basically psychological and should convey an understanding of humanity. When this type of training is given, we shall develop men and women who are both civilised and cultured and who will also possess the capacity to move forward (as life unfolds) into that world of meaning which underlies the world of outer phenomena and who will begin to view human happenings in terms of the deeper spiritual and universal values.

Education should be the process whereby youth is taught to reason from cause to effect, to know the reason why certain actions are bound inevitably to produce certain results and why (given a certain emotional and mental equipment, plus an ascertained psychological rating) definite life trends can be determined and certain professions and life careers provide the right setting for development and a useful and profitable field of experience. Some attempts along this line have been undertaken by certain colleges and schools in an effort to ascertain the psychological aptitudes of a boy or a girl for certain vocations but the whole effort is still amateurish in nature. When made more scientific it opens the door for training in the sciences; it gives significance and meaning to history, biography and learning and thus avoids the bare impartation of facts and the crude process of memory training which has been distinctive of past methods.

The new education will consider a child with due reference to his heredity, his social position, his national conditioning, his environment and his individual mental and emotional equipment and will seek to throw the entire world of effort open to him, pointing out that apparent barriers to progress are only spurs to renewed endeavour and thus seeking to "lead him out" (the true meaning of the word "education") from any limiting condition and train him to think in terms of constructive world citizenship. Growth and still more growth will be emphasised.

The educator of the future will approach the problem of youth from the angle of the *instinctual* reaction of the children, their *intellectual* capacity and and their *intuitional* potentiality. In infancy and in the earlier school grades, the development of right instinctual reactions will be watched and cultivated; in the later grades, in what is equivalent to the high schools or the secondary schools, the intellectual unfoldment and control of the mental processes will be emphasised, whilst in the colleges and universities the unfoldment of the intuition, the importance of ideals and ideas and the development of abstract thinking and perception will be fostered; this latter phase will be soundly based upon the previous sound intellectual foundation. These three factors—instinct, intellect and intuition—provide the keynotes for the three scholastic institutions through which every young person will pass and through which, today, many thousands do pass.

In the future, education will make a far wider use of psychology than heretofore. A trend in this direction is definitely to be seen. The nature—physical, vital, emotional and mental—of the boy or girl will be carefully investigated and his incoherent life purposes directed along right lines; he will be taught to recognise himself as the one who acts, who feels and who thinks. Thus the responsibility of the central "I," or the occupant of the body will be taught. This will alter the entire present attitude of the youth of the world to their surroundings and foster, from the earliest days, the recognition of a part to be played and a responsibility to be assumed and that education is a method of preparation for that useful and interesting future.

It, therefore, becomes increasingly apparent that the coming education could be defined in a new and broader sense as the Science of Right Human Relations and of Social Organisation. This gives a comparatively new purpose to any curriculum imparted and yet indicates that nothing hitherto included need be excluded, only a better motivation will be obvious and a nationalistic, selfish presentation avoided. If history is, for instance, presented on the basis of the conditioning ideas which have led humanity onward and not on the basis of aggressive wars and international or national thievery, then education will concern itself with the right perception and use of ideas, of their transformation into working ideals and their application as the will-to-good, the will-to-truth and the will-to-beauty. Thus a much needed alteration of humanity's aims from our present competitive and materialistic objectives into those that will more fully express the Golden Rule will come about and right relations between individuals, groups, parties, nations and throughout the entire international world will be established.

Increasingly, education should be concerned with the

wholes of life as well as with the details of daily individual living. The child, as an individual, will be developed and equipped, trained and motivated and taught then his responsibilities to the whole and the value of the contribution which he can and must make to the group.

It is perhaps a platitude to say that education should occupy itself necessarily with the development of the reasoning powers of the child and not primarily—as is now usually the case—with the training of the memory and the parrot-like recording of facts and dates and uncorrelated and ill-digested items of information. The history of the growth of man's perceptive faculties under differing national and racial conditions is of profound interest. The outstanding figures of history, literature and art and of religion will surely be studied from the angle of their effort and their influence for good or evil upon their period; the quality and purpose of their leadership will be considered. Thus the child will absorb a vast amount of historical information, of creative activity and of idealism and philosophy not only with the maximum of ease but with permanent effect upon his character.

The continuity of effort, the effects upon civilisation of ancient tradition, good and evil happenings and the interplay of varying cultural aspects of civilisation will be brought to his attention and the dry-as-dust information, dates and names will fall into the discard. All branches of human knowledge could, in this way, become alive and reach a new level of constructive usefulness. There is already a definite tendency in this direction and it is good and sound. The past of humanity as the foundation for present happenings and the present as the determining factor for the future, will increasingly be recognised and thus great and needed changes will be brought about in human psychology as a whole.

The creative aptitude of the human being should also, under the new era, receive fuller attention; the child will be spurred on to individual effort suited to his temperament and capacity. Thus he will be induced to contribute what he can of beauty to the world and of right thought to the sumtotal of human thinking; he will be encouraged to investigate and the world of science will open up before him. Behind all these applied incentives, the motives of goodwill and right human relations will be found.

Finally, education should surely present the hypothesis of the soul in man as the interior factor which produces the good, the true and the beautiful. Creative expression and humanitarian effort will, therefore, receive a logical basis. This will not be done through a theological or doctrinal presentation, as is today the case, but as presenting a problem for investigation and as an effort to answer the question: What is man; what is his intrinsic purpose in the scheme of things? The livingness of the influence and the proclaimed purpose behind the constant appearance of spiritual, cultural and artistic world leaders down the ages will be studied and their lives subjected to research, both historical and psychological. This will open up before the youth of the world the entire problem of leadership and of motive. Education will, therefore, be given in the form of human interest, human achievement and human possibility. This will be done in such a manner that the content of the student's mind will not only be enriched with historical and literary facts but his imagination will be fired, and his ambition and aspiration evoked along true and right lines; the world of past human effort will be presented to him in a truer perspective and the future thrown open to him also in an appeal for his individual effort and personal contribution.

What I have written above in no way implies an indictment of past methods except in so far that the world today itself presents an indictment; it does not either constitute an impractical vision or a mystical hope, based on wishful thinking. It concerns an attitude to life and the future which many thousands of people hold today, and among them many, many educators in every country. The errors and mistakes of the past techniques are obvious but there is no need to waste time in emphasising them or in piling up instances. What is needed is a realisation of the immediate opportunity, plus the recognition that the required shift in objectives and change in methods will take much time. We shall have to train our teachers differently and much time will be lost as we grope for the new and better ways, develop the new textbooks and find the men and women who can be impressed with the new vision and who will work for the new civilisation. I have sought only to emphasise principles and I do this with the recognition that many of them are by no means new but that they require new emphasis. I have endeavoured to show that now is the day of opportunity, for everything has to be built up again, for everything has been destroyed in the greater part of the world. The war has demonstrated that we have not taught aright. A better educational system should, therefore, be worked out which will present the possibilities of human living in such a manner that barriers will be broken down, prejudices removed and a training given to the developing child which will enable him, when grownup, to live with other men in harmony and goodwill. This *can* be done, if patience and understanding are developed and if educators realise that "where there is no vision, the people perish."

An international system of education, developed in joint conference by broadminded teachers and educational authorities in every country, is today a crying need and would provide a major asset in preserving world peace. Steps towards this are already being taken and today groups of educators are getting together and discussing the formation of a better system which will guarantee that the children of the different nations (beginning with the millions of children now demanding education) will be taught truth, without bias or prejudice. World democracy will take form when men everywhere are regarded in reality as equal; when boys and g'rls are taught that it does not matter whether a man is an Asiatic, an American, a European, British, a Jew or a Gentile but only that each has an historical background and history which enables him to contribute something to the good of the whole, and that the major requirement is an attitude of goodwill and a constant effort to foster right human relations. World Unity will be a fact when the children of the world are taught that religious differences are largely a matter of birth; that if a man is born in Italy, the probability is that he will be a Roman Catholic; if he is born a Jew, he will follow the Jewish teaching; if born in Asia, he may be a Mohammedan, a Buddhist, or belong to one of the Hindu sects; if born in other countries, he may be a Protestant and so on. He will learn that the religious differences are largely the result of man made quarrels over human interpretations of truth. Thus gradually, our quarrels and differences will be offset and the idea of the One Humanity will take their place.

Much greater care will have to be given in picking and training the teachers of the future. Their mental attainments and their knowledge of their particular subject will be of importance, but more important still will be the need for them to be free from prejudice and to see all men as members of a great family. The educator of the future will need to be more of a trained psychologist than he is today. Besides imparting academic knowledge, he will realise that his major task is to evoke out of his class of students a real sense of responsibility; no matter what he has to teach—history, geography, mathematics, languages, science in its various branches or philosophy—he will relate it all to the Science of Right Human Relations and try to give a truer perspective than in the past upon social organisation.

When the young people of the future—under the proposed application of principles—are civilised, cultured and responsive to world citizenship, we shall have a world of men awakened, creative and possessing a true sense of values and a sound and constructive outlook on world affairs. It will take a long time to bring this about, but it is not impossible as history itself has proved.

It will be only common sense, however, to realise that this integration is not possible for every student passing through the hands of our teachers. All, however, no matter what their initial capacity, can be trained in the Science of Right Human Relations and thus respond to the major objective of the coming educational systems. Indications of this can be seen on every hand but as yet the emphasis is *not* laid on it when training teachers or influencing parents. Much, very much, has been done by enlightened groups of men in all lands and this they have done whilst studying the requirements for citizenship, whilst undertaking research work connected with correct social relations (communal, national and international) and through the many organisations which are trying to bring to the mass of human beings a sense of responsibility for human happiness and human welfare. Nevertheless, the real work along these lines should be started in infancy so that the consciousness of the child (so easily directed) can from its earliest days assume an unselfish attitude towards his associates. It can be started very simply if the parents so desire; it can be carried forward progressively if parents and teachers demonstrate in their own lives what they teach. Finally the time will come, under these conditions, when in late adolescence a crisis, needed and planned, is precipitated in the young person's life, and he will then stabilise himself in the particular manner in which destiny ordains that he shall fulfil his task of right relationship through the means of *vocational service*.

It is bridging work which has now to be done—bridging between what is today and what can be in the future. If, during the next 150 years, we develop this technique of bridging the many cleavages found in the human family and in offsetting the racial hatreds and the separative attitudes of nations and people, we shall have succeeded in implementing a world in which war will be impossible and humanity will be realising itself as one human family and not as a fighting aggregate of many nations and people, competitively engaged in getting the best of each other and successfully fostering prejudices and hatred. This has, as we have seen, been the history of the past. Man has been developed from an isolated animal, prompted only by the instincts of self-preservation, eating, and mating, through the stages of family life, tribal life and national life to the point where today a still broader ideal is grasped by him—international unity or the smooth functioning of the One Humanity. This growing idealism is fighting its way into the forefront of the human consciousness in spite of all separative enmities. It is largely responsible for the present chaos and for the banding together of the United Nations. It has produced the conflicting ideologies which are seeking world expression; it has produced the dramatic emergence of national saviours (so-called), world prophets and world workers, idealists, opportunists, dictators, investigators and humanitarians. These conflicting idealisms are a wholesome sign, whether we agree with them or not. They are definitely exploiting the human demand—urgent and right—for better conditions, for more light and understanding, for greater cooperation, for security and peace and plenty in the place of terror, fear and starvation.

It is difficult for modern man to conceive of a time when there will be no racial, national or separative religious consciousness present in human thinking. It was equally difficult for prehistoric man to conceive of a time when there would be national thinking and this is a good thing for us to bear in mind. The time when humanity will be able to think in universal terms still lies far ahead but the fact that we can speak of it, desire it and plan for it is surely the guarantee that it is *not* impossible. Humanity has always progressed from stage to stage of enlightenment and from glory to glory. We are today on our way to a far better civilisation than the world has ever known and towards conditions which will ensure a much happier humanity and which will see the end of national differences, of class distinctions (whether based on an hereditary or a financial status) and which will ensure a fuller and richer life for everyone.

It will be obvious that very many decades must elapse before such a state of affairs will be actively present—but it will be decades and not centuries, if humanity can learn the lessons of war and if the reactionary and the conservative peoples in every nation can be prevented from swinging civilisation back on to the bad old lines. But a beginning can immediately be made. Simplicity should be our watchword for it is simplicity which will kill our old materialistic way of living. *Cooperative goodwill* is surely the first idea to be presented to the masses and taught in our schools, thereby guaranteeing the new and better civilisation. *Loving understanding,* intelligently applied, should be the hallmark of the cultured and wiser groups, plus effort on their part to relate the world of meaning to the world of outer efforts —for the benefit of the masses. *World Citizenship* as an expression of both goodwill and understanding should be the goal of the enlightened everywhere and the hallmark of the spiritual man, and in these three, you have right relations established between education, religion and politics.

All the work being done now is definitely transitional work and therefore most difficult. It infers a bridging process between the old and the new, and would present almost insuperable difficulties were it not for the fact that the coming two generations will bring in those types of egos who are competent to deal with the problem. Upon this fact those of you who are concerned with the educational system and situation, and who are bewildered by the presented vision and by the task of approximating the cherished possibilities, must rest back with confidence. Clear thinking, much love and a sense of true compromise (note this phrase) will do much to lay the needed foundations and keep the door of the future wide open. A balancing process is going forward in this interim period, and to it the modern educator should pay due attention.

I can perhaps indicate the nature of this process. I have stated here and elsewhere that the soul anchors itself in the body at two points:

1. There is a thread of energy, which we call the life or spirit aspect, anchored in the heart. It uses the blood stream, as is well known, as its distributing agency and, through the medium of the blood, life-energy carries regenerating power and coordinating energy to all the physical organisms and keeps the body "whole."

2. There is a thread of energy, which we call the consciousness aspect or the faculty of soul knowledge, anchored in the centre of the head. It controls that response mechanism which we call the brain, and through its medium it directs activity and induces awareness throughout the body by means of the nervous system.

These two energy factors, which are recognised by human beings as life and knowledge, or as living energy and intelligence, are the two poles of a child's being. The task ahead of him is to develop consciously the middle or balancing aspect which is love or *group relationship,* in order that knowledge should be subordinated to the group need and interests, and that living energy should be turned consciously and with intention into the group *whole.* In doing this a true balance will be achieved and it will be brought about by the recognition that the *Way of Service* is a scientific technique for the achieving of this balance. Educators therefore have three things to bear in mind during this present period of transition:

1. To reorient the knowledge, the consciousness aspect
    or the sense of awareness in the child in such a manner
    that he realises from infancy that all that he has been
    taught or is being taught is with the view to the good
    of others more than of himself. He will therefore be
    trained to be definitely forward looking. Information
    as to the past history of the race will be given to him
    from the angle of the racial growth in consciousness
    and not so much from the angle of the *facts* of mate-
    rial or aggressive achievement as is now the case. As
    the past, in the child's mind, is correlated with the
    present, his capacity to correlate, unify and bridge, in
    the different aspects of his life and on various planes,
    will be developed.

2. To teach him that the life which he feels pulsing
    through his veins is only one small part of the total
    life pulsing throughout all forms, all kingdoms in
    nature, all planets, and the solar system. He will learn
    that he shares it with all that exists, and that there-
    fore a true "blood Brotherhood" is everywhere to
    be found. Consequently, from the very start of his
    life, he can be taught *relationship,* and this the small
    child will be apt to recognise more quickly than will
    the average adult, trained in the ways and attitudes
    of the old age. When these two realisations—respon-
    sibility and relationship—are inculcated in the child
    from infancy, then the third objective of the new ed-
    ucation will come with greater ease.

3. The unification in consciousness of the life impulse
    and the urge to knowledge will lead eventually to a
    planned activity. This planned activity will consti-
    tute service, and this, in its turn, will do three things
    for the child who is taught to practice it:

    a. It will serve as a directional agency from the earli-
        est years, finally indicating vocation and avocation
        and thus aiding in the choice of a life career.

b. It will draw out the best that is in the child and will make him a magnetic radiating centre in the place where he is. It will enable him to attract to himself those who can help him or be helped by him, those who can serve him and whom he best can serve.

c. It will therefore make him definitely *creative,* and so enable him to spin that thread of energy which, when added to the life thread and to the consciousness thread, will link head, heart and throat into one unified and functioning agency.

The meeting of the three aforesaid requirements will be the primary step (made on a racial scale) to the building of the antahkarana or the bridge between:

1. Various aspects of the form nature.
2. The personality and the soul.
3. The man and other human beings.
4. The man as a member of the human family, and his environing world.

You will note from this that education should be basically concerned with relations and interrelations, with the bridging or the healing of cleavages, and thus with the restoration of unity or synthesis. The establishment of the Science of Right Relations is the next immediate step in the mental unfoldment of the race. It is the major activity of the new education.

THE AQUARIAN AGE

As a result of the bridging work which will be done in the immediate one hundred and fifty years ahead of us, the technique of bridging the various cleavages found in the human family, and of weaving into one strong cable the various threads of energy which tenuously, as yet, connect the various aspects of the inner man with the outer form, will have made so much progress that the bulk of the intelligent people in the world and of all classes and nations will be integrated personalities. When this is the case, the science of the antahkarana will be a planned part of their training. Today, as we study this science and its related sciences of meditation and service, the appeal will be only to the world aspirants and disciples. Its usefulness will only be found at present to be for those special incarnating souls who are today coming into incarnation with such rapidity as a response to the world's need for help. But later the appeal will be general and its usefulness more nearly universal.

It is needless for me to outline for you the nature of the educational systems of the Aquarian Age because they would prove most unsuitable at this time. I mention them as it is necessary to remember that the work done during the next two centuries in the field of education is definitely temporary and balancing, and that out of the fulfillment of the task assigned to education will grow those more permanent systems which, in the new age, will be found flourishing everywhere.

Three major sciences will eventually dominate the field of education in the new age. They will not negate the activities of modern science but will integrate them into a wider subjective whole. These three sciences are:

1. *The Science of the Antahkarana.* This is the new and true science of the mind, which will utilise mental substance for the building of the bridge between personality and soul, and then between the soul and the spiritual triad. This constitutes active work in substance subtler than the substance of the three worlds of ordinary human evolution. It concerns the substance of the three higher levels of the mental plane. These symbolic bridges, when constructed, will facilitate the stream or flow of consciousness and will produce that continuity of consciousness, or that sense of unimpeded awareness, which will finally end the fear of death,

negate all sense of separateness, and make a man responsive in his brain consciousness to impressions coming to him from the higher spiritual realms or from the Mind of God. Thus he will more easily be initiated into the purposes and plans of the Creator.

2. *The Science of Meditation.* At present meditation is associated in the minds of men with religious matters. But that relates only to theme. The science can be applied to every possible life process. In reality, this science is a subsidiary branch, preparatory to the Science of the Antahkarana. It is really the true science of occult bridge building or bridging in consciousness. By its means, particularly in the early stages, the building process is facilitated. It is one of the major ways of spiritual functioning; it is one of the many ways to God; it relates the individual mind eventually to the higher mind and later to the Universal Mind. It is one of the major building techniques and will eventually dominate the new educational methods in schools and colleges. It is intended primarily to:

a. Produce sensitivity to the higher impressions.

b. Build the first half of the antahkarana, that between the personality and the soul.

c. Produce an eventual continuity of consciousness. Meditation is essentially the science of light, because it works in the substance of light. One branch of it is concerned with the science of visualisation because, as the light continues to bring revelation, the power to visualise can grow with the aid of the illumined mind, and the later work of training the disciple to create is then made possible. It might be added here that the building of the second half of the antahkarana (that which bridges the gap in consciousness between the soul and the spiritual triad) is called the science of vision, because just as the first half of the bridge is built through the use of mental substance, so the second half is built through the use of light substance.

3. *The Science of Service* grows normally and naturally out of the successful application of the other two sciences. As the linking up of soul and personality proceeds, and as the knowledge of the plan and the light of the soul pour into the brain consciousness, the normal result is the subordination of the lower to the higher. Identification with group purposes and plans is the natural attribute of the soul. As this identification is carried forward on mental and soul levels, it produces a corresponding activity in the personal life and this activity we call service. Service is the true science of creation and is a scientific method of establishing continuity.

These three sciences will be regarded eventually as the three major concerns of the educational process and upon them will the emphasis increasingly be placed.

We have now laid the ground for a consideration of the three sciences which will dominate the thought of educators in the coming age. The building and the development of the antahkarana, the development of the power to control life and to work white magic through the science of meditation, and also the science of service whereby group control and group relationship are fostered and developed—these are the three fundamental sciences which will guide the psychologist and the educator of the future. These will also cause a radical change in the attitude of parents towards their children and in the methods which they employ to train and teach them when they are very young and in the formative years of their consciousness.

It should here be remembered that these parents themselves will have been brought up under this new and different regime and will themselves have been developed under this changed mode of approaching the educational process. What may therefore seem to you mystical and vague (because of its newness, or its idealism and its emphasis upon a seeming abstract group consciousness), will seem to them normal and natural. What I am here outlining to you is a possibility which lies ahead for the next two or three generations; I am also referring to a recognition which a new educational ideology will normally permit to govern the mode of instruction.

CHAPTER IV

The Culture of the Individual

THE CULTURE of the individual will be approached from three angles, each contributing to the completed whole which is to make the individual: an intelligent citizen of two worlds (the world of objective existence and the inner world of meaning), a wise parent, a controlled and directed personality. We shall now proceed to take up these points.

I have not elaborated the teaching of the Aquarian Age nor dealt at all with the educational systems of that time. It is of no service to you to do so, and I am unable to really aid your thought if I jump you forward two hundred years into a civilisation and a culture of which, as yet, only the faintest indications can be seen. It is of more value if I lay the emphasis upon the emerging ideas which will govern future procedure in the next generation and carry the world through the most difficult transitional period which it has ever seen.

Certain basic ideals, emerging out of the current ideologies, are beginning to make their impact upon public consciousness. These ideals in themselves are essentially human reactions to divine ideas; they are consequently not entirely free from error and are necessarily coloured by the calibre of the minds which are formulating them; they are inevitably conditioned by past history, by national tradition and by racial trends of thought. There is, nevertheless, a curious uniformity about them, even when expressed by the fol-

lowers of widely diverging world idealism. If we are
properly to understand these ideas and are to lay a right
foundation, it would be of value perhaps if we discussed
some of these universal attitudes and considered what they
indicate in the light of the present world problems, and the
indications of the coming world which we can draw there-
from.

THE ANGLE OF CITIZENSHIP

There is a growing feeling amongst the citizens of most
nations that the major task of the educational systems is to
fit the child for citizenship. By that they mean that it is the
task of the State and of the taxpayers so to train the child
that he may be a cooperative, intelligent part of that organised whole which we call a nation; that he may be so disci-
plined that he can take his part in and make his contribution
to the State and thus can be of social value yet play a distinct individual part, and at the same time a group-directed
part, in the life of the community wherein he has been born
and in which he must necessarily sustain himself; that his
individual life and interests count less than the corporate life,
and that the preliminary lesson he must be taught is the fact
that he is a unit in a functioning group of similar units,
each of whom is expected to contribute his quota of good
to the whole.

The initial germ of this idea (amazing as it may seem)
started when the first school was organised, thousands of
years ago. These schools were very small at first, educating
oniy a favoured few, but leading up gradually (usually via
religious organisations) to that mass education and compulsory tuition which distinguishes the modern State schools,
whose task it noticeably is to prepare millions of young
people in the world for intelligent, but directed, citizenship.

Today, among the so-called enlightened nations, some
kind of compulsory education is imposed upon the masses;
the children of all nations are taught reading, writing and

the rudiments of arithmetic. They are supposed thereby to have a general idea of world conditions—taught geographically, historically and economically—and are supposed thereby to achieve some recognition, objectively and naturally, of the processes and reasons why the various nations have come to be what they are and where they are, and so to have gained a consciousness of a general planetary picture. The changing outlines of this picture are today producing mental flexibility in children, and this is, in many ways, a definite asset.

In producing citizens, however, the emphasis up till this time has been twofold. The aim of education has been so to equip the child that when he reached years of maturity he could take care of himself in the predatory world of modern life, earn a livelihood and become if possible rich and independent of those with whom his life was cast. In all this tuitional process the emphasis was laid upon himself as an individual, and the point of interest was upon what *he* was going to do, how *he* was going to live, and what *he* could get, make and achieve out of life.

In those conditions where the school bias was religious (as in Church schools of any kind), he was taught that he must endeavour to be good, and the selfish incentive was held before him that if he could do this he might some day go to Heaven and have a happy time. When these ideas had been instilled into him, when he had been forced by organisational pressure into the desired pattern and mould, when he had absorbed the needed amount of sketchy information about humanity and human achievements, and when his capacity to remember facts (historical, scientific, religious and other) had been developed, even though his power to think remained entirely undeveloped, he was turned loose upon the world and his ordained community to make good and to establish *himself*.

The above is, I realise, a broad generalisation. It leaves out of reckoning altogether the innate and inherent capacities of the child, his achieved point of soul development, and any recognition of the powers with which he enters into life as a result of many previous life experiences. It leaves out also the influence of the many conscientious, spiritually-minded and highly evolved teachers who have— down the ages—set their mark upon the young people they have taught and thus oriented them and led them forward to better things. I am dealing solely with the institutional aspect of the educational systems and with the proven effect upon the young of every nation who have been subjected to these systems. The realised goals which the institutional teacher has set before himself have been narrow, and the consequent effect of his teaching and of his work has been the production of a selfish, materialistically-minded person whose major objective has been self-betterment in a material sense. This has been strikingly aided where any individual ambition has been present which would lead the child to operate willingly with the narrow selfish goal of the teacher. The natural idealism of the child (and what child is not an innate idealist?) has been slowly and steadily suffocated by the weight of the materialism of the world's educational machine and by the selfish bias of the world's business in its many departments, plus the emphasis always laid upon the necessity of making money.

Little by little this disastrous state of affairs (which reached its climax in the early years of this century) has been slowly changing, so that today in many countries the welfare of the State itself, the good of the Empire, the need of the Nation is held before the child from its earliest years as the highest possible ideal. He is taught that he must serve the State, Empire, or Nation with the very best that is in him; it is strongly inculcated into his consciousness that his individual life must be subordinated to the greater life of the State or Nation, and that it is his duty to meet the national need, even at the expense of life itself. He is taught that in times of great emergency he, as an individual, does not count at all, but that the larger corporate whole, of which he is an infinitesimal part, is the sole factor that matters. This is a definite step forward in the expansion of consciousness which the human race must achieve.

I would here remind you that it is the expansion of consciousness and the production of increased sensitivity and perceptive awareness which is the goal of all divine and hierarchical effort. The goal is not for betterment of material conditions. These will automatically follow when the sense of awareness is steadily unfolded. The future of humanity is determined by its aspiration and ability to respond to the idealism which is today flooding the world.

At this time also a still further step is taking place. Everywhere and in every country men are being taught in their earliest years that they are not only individuals, not only members of a state, empire or nation, and not only people with an individual future, but that they are intended to be exponents of certain great group ideologies—Democratic, Totalitarian, or Communistic. These ideologies are, in the last analysis, materialising dreams or visions. For these, modern youth is taught that he must work and strive and, if necessary, fight. It is therefore surely apparent that behind all the surface turmoil and chaos so devastatingly present today in the consciousness of humanity, and behind all the fear and apprehension, the hate and separativeness, human beings are beginning to blend in themselves three states of consciousness—that of the individual, of the citizen, and of the idealist. The power to achieve this, and to be all these states simultaneously, is now reaching down into those levels of human life which we call "submerged classes."

All this is very good and part of the ordained plan. Whether it is the democratic ideal, or the vision of the totalitarian state, or the dream of the communistic devotee, the effect upon the consciousness of humanity as a whole is definitely good. His sense of world awareness is definitely growing, his power to regard himself as part of a whole is rapidly developing and all this is desirable and right and contained within the divine plan.

It is of course entirely true that the process is spoiled and handicapped by methods and motives that are highly undesirable, but human beings have a habit of spoiling that which is beautiful; they have a highly developed capacity of being selfish and material, and because the minds of men are as yet practically untrained and undeveloped, they have little power of discrimination and small ability to differentiate between the old and the new, or between the right and the more right. Having been trained in selfishness and in material attitudes while under parental control and in the educational systems of the day, their trend of thought normally runs along these undesirable lines.

In the Piscean Age which is passing, the youth in every country has been brought up under the influence of three foundational ideas. The result of these ideas might be expressed under the terms of the following questions:

1. What shall be my vocation in order that I may have as much of the material world as my state in life and my wants permit?

2. Who are the people who are above me, to whom I must look and whom I must honor, and who are those below me in the social order and how far am I able to mount in the social scale and so better myself?

3. From childhood I have been taught that my natural inclination is to do wrong, to be naughty, or (if the setting is narrowly orthodox) that I am a miserable sinner and unfit for future happiness. How can I escape the penalties of my natural predilections?

The result of all this is to breed in the race a deep-seated sense of material and social ambition and also an inferiority complex which necessarily breaks out into some form of revolt in the individual, in racial explosions or, again speaking individually, in a rabidly self-centered attitude to life. From these distorted tendencies and retrogressive ideals the race must eventually emerge. It is the realisation of this which has produced in some nations the overemphasis on the national or racial good and on the State as an entity. It has led to the undermining of the hierarchical structure of the social order. This hierarchical structure is a basic and eternal reality, but the concept has been so distorted and so misused that it has evoked a revolt in humanity and has produced an almost abnormal reaction to a freedom and a license which are assuming undesirable dimensions.

The widespread demand of the youth of the world today (in some countries) for a good time, their irresponsibility and their refusal to face the real values of life, are all indicative of this. This is to be seen at its worst in the democratic countries. In the totalitarian states it is not permitted on the same scale, as the youth in those states are forced to shoulder responsibility and to dedicate themselves to the larger whole, and not to a life of material vocation and the wasting of their years in what I believe you slangfully call "a good time." This good time is usually had at the expense of others, and takes place in the formative years which inevitably condition and determine the young person's future.

I am not here speaking politically or in defense of any governmental system. A forced activity and then a forced responsibility, relegate the bulk of those so conditioned to the nursery stage or the child state, and humanity should be reaching maturity, with its willingness to shoulder responsibility and its growing sense of the real values of the standards of life. The sense of responsibility is one of the first indications that the soul of the individual is awakened.

The soul of humanity is also at this time awakening en masse, and hence the following indications:

1. The growth of societies, organisations and mass movements for the betterment of humanity everywhere.
2. The growing interest of the mass of the people in the common welfare. Hitherto the upper layer of society has been interested, either for selfish, self-protective reasons or because of innate paternalism. The intelligentsia and the professional classes have investigated and studied the public welfare from the angle of mental and scientific interest, based upon a general material basis, and the lower middle class has naturally been involved in the same interest, from the point of view of financial and trade returns. Today this interest has reached down to the depths of the social orcer and all classes are keenly alive and alert to the general, national, racial or international good. This is very well and a hopeful sign.
3. Humanitarian and philanthropic effort is at its height, alongside of the cruelties, hatreds and abnormalities which separativeness, overstressed national ideologies, aggressiveness and ambition have engendered in the life of all nations.
4. Education is rapidly becoming mass effort and the children of all nations from the highest to the lowest are being intellectually equipped as never before. The effort is, of course, largely to enable them to meet material and national conditions, to be of use to the State and no economic drag upon it. The general result is, however, in line with the divine plan and undoubtedly good.
5. The growing recognition by those in authority that the man in the street is becoming a factor in world affairs. He is reached on all sides by the press and the radio, and is today intelligent enough and in-

terested enough to be making the attempt to form his own opinions and come to his own conclusions. This is embryonic as yet, but the indications of his effort are undoubtedly there; hence the press and radio control which is found in all countries in some form or another, for there can never be any permanent evasion of the hierarchical structure which underlies our planetary life. This control falls into two major categories:

Financial control, as in the United States.

Government control, as in Europe and Great Britain.

The people are told just what is good for them; reservations and secret diplomacy colour the relation of the government to the masses, and the helplessness of the man in the street (in the face of authorities in the realm of politics, conditioning decisions such as war or peace, and theological impositions, as well as economic attitudes) is still pitiful, though not so great and so drastic as it was. The soul of humanity is awakening and the present situations may be regarded as temporary.

The purpose of the coming educational systems will be to preserve individual integrity, promote the sense of individual responsibility, encourage a developing group consciousness of basic individual, national and world relationships, meanwhile extroverting and organising capacity, interest and ability. At the same time there will be an effort to intensify the sense of citizenship, both in the tangible outer world of the physical plane and in the Kingdom of God and of soul relationships.

In order to bring this about, and thus completely change the present world attitudes and wrong emphases, the drastic and catastrophic present planetary situation has been permitted.

THE WORLD SITUATION AND IDEOLOGIES

Before we take up the more technical side of our work, I would have you for a moment reflect upon the world situation and the world ideologies from the angle of education. I would have you consider it deeply from the point of view of the existing fundamental group relations, envisaging the necessity to prepare the youth of the future for the coming age—outlines of which can only now dimly be seen. I would like you to achieve if possible a general idea of the present world situation, dealing only with the broad and general outlines and omitting any study of detail or of specific personalities, except by way of illustration. In my other writings I have laid a foundation for this when I briefly endeavoured to consider the psychological problem of the various nations, its cause or causes, and the peculiar contribution which each specific nation has to make to the world whole.

We will try to recognise certain outstanding facts, though these facts may be more usually considered facts by esotericists than by the world in general. But we are working, or endeavouring to work, as esotericists. These facts are:

1. The fact that there are certain basic ideas which have come forth down the ages and have brought humanity to its present evolutionary point. Ideas are the substance of the evolutionary urge.

2. The fact that there is a hidden control which has persisted down the ages and which can be deduced from the definitely emerging plan, as far as the consciousness of man is concerned.

3. The fact that all growth is through experiment, struggle and persistence—hence the present modern upheaval. It is significant of a "pushing through" to the light, the light of the world, as well as the group antahkarana.

It is obvious that a good deal of what I may give in these instructions may not prove of immediate application, but students are asked to ponder and to think along the lines which I may point out, for only as a nucleus of thinkers is thus formed who are responsive to the new educational ideas, does it become possible for the spiritual Hierarchy of Masters to achieve the intended results in Their work to bring into being the plans of God. The Masters can not and do not work without Their chosen physical plane focal points. I would ask you again to regard yourselves as outposts of the consciousness of Those Who, upon the inner side of life, are seeking to bring in new light upon the subject of social organisations, the relationship of the individual to the whole, and the new and desirable trends in education. I would ask you to submit yourselves to thought training with this in view. Note the manner in which I have worded this request: first, regard; then, train. First, faith as to contact; then the steps taken to facilitate and develop that contact.

Our theme is the study of the educational organisation of humanity, involving as it does (in its later stages) responsibility and right action. We shall consider, on broad lines, the development of man from an isolated personal unit, through the stages of family life, tribal life, national life, to the present stage of aspirational idealistic humanity. This idealism and this prevalent enquiry are responsible for the present world chaos; they have produced the conflicting ideologies, and the dramatic emergence of the national saviours, world prophets and workers, idealists, opportunists, dictators and investigators on all sides, in every department of human thought and in every land. This idealism is a good sign. It is also responsible for the seething unrest and the urgent demand for better conditions, more light and understanding, deepened cooperation, for a security based on right adjustments, and for peace and plenty in the place of fear, terror and starvation.

It is not my intention to handle this subject from the angle of the many modern textbooks on government, on law, or on the many schemes (economic, political, etc.) which are today so dominantly engrossing attention. I do not intend to go into details or definitions. The exponents of the differing creeds can provide the needed literature and present their case far more successfully than I can. The protagonists of an ideology can express their beliefs and objectives more fervently and hopefully than is possible to me. I shall write for you as one who sees the pattern emerging more clearly than you, because I can see it both from the inside and the outside, and also from the blueprints in the custody of the Hierarchy. I shall write as one who has, in conference with workers in the Hierarchy, sought to comprehend the objectives and to cooperate with the immediate plans in this time of planetary crisis and upheaval, of drastic changes, and of the stepping up of humanity to new levels of living and higher states of consciousness; as one who has studied somewhat deeply into the records of the past and into the modes of meditation, and has achieved thereby a measure of inclusiveness of past, present and future which is naturally not possible for you at this time.

Some of the plans and ideas controlling hierarchical action I will seek to lay before you, leaving them to ferment in your minds, thus bringing to you either rejection or conviction. I but seek to suggest. It is for you to make deduction, to draw intelligent inferences, and to *think* along the lines indicated. I seek to have you steep yourselves in this line of thought so that my work with your minds may be facilitated and the group building of the needed bridges of light may go on apace. Forget not that I, too, have to make an effort to render my thought and ideas intelligible to you, and this can only be possible if *I* demonstrate wisdom and *you* demonstrate intelligence and perseverance. Where the teacher is wise and the pupil intelligent, much then becomes possible.

I would ask that your attitude should also be (for a time at least) non-critical; that you discard temporarily your preconceived ideas; that you cultivate a willingness to consider and to weigh, not evidence this time, but an inner structure of esoteric happening of more import than the outer events, and thus grasp somewhat of *the purpose of the new education.* Ponder on this last phrase and deeply consider my meaning. I would have you achieve a vertical position, with a horizontal outlook. Ponder too on this phrase.

As we study the way of man as he gropes his way out of the animal condition to his present increasingly intellectual attitude, and as he presses forward into a future of widest possibility and opportunity, let us always remember that to the Custodians of God's Plan and to Those Who are working out the new developments, *the form side of life,* the outer tangible expression, is of entirely secondary importance. Your vision is oft distorted by the pain and suffering to which the form is subjected (either your own or that of others, individually or en masse), so that you do not see clearly the purpose and the urgency of *the life within the form.* To many of you, for instance, the World War was a supreme disaster, an agony to be averted in the future at any cost, a dire and dreadful happening indicative of the wickedness of man and the incredible blind indifference of God. To us, on the inner side, the World War was in the nature of a major surgical operation made in an effort to save the patient's life. A violent streptococcic germ and infection had menaced the life of humanity (speaking in symbols) and an operation was made in order to prolong opportunity and save life, *not* to save the form. This operation was largely successful. The germ, to be sure, is not eradicated and makes its presence felt in infected areas in the body of humanity.

Another surgical operation may be necessary, not in order to destroy and end the present civilisation, but in order to dissipate the infection and get rid of the fever. It may not, however, be needed, for a process of dissipation, distribution and absorption has been going on and may prove effective. Let us work towards that end. But at the same time, let us never forget that it is the *Life,* its purpose and its directed intentional destiny that is of importance; and also that when a form proves inadequate, or too diseased, or too crippled for the expression of that purpose, it is—from the point of view of the Hierarchy—no disaster when that form has to go. Death is not a disaster to be feared; the work of the Destroyer is not really cruel or undesirable. I say this to you who am myself upon the Ray of Love and know its meaning.

There are two lines of destruction: that which is meted out by human beings with no understanding of the life purposes, who act blindly and ignorantly, prompted by selfish desire, by love of power or by hatred; there is also that which is permitted by the soul in due and right time, and it comes when a new vehicle of expression is demanded by the indwelling life. Therefore, there is much destruction permitted by the Custodians of the Plan and much evil turned into good, because the end is seen from the beginning, and the consciousness is ripe enough in experience to relinquish the form because of the sensed benefits to be gained. This is true of individuals, of nations and of races. Sensitivity to world suffering is a great and divine characteristic; when, however, it is qualified by emotion, it becomes separative in interpretation and focussed in partisanship and personalities, and thus develops into a glamour and an illusion, confusing the real issue and blinding men to the divine facts.

I would remind you that the esotericist always argues from universals to particulars. This I shall always do, and thus offset the detailed point of view, the distorted foreground and the myopic vision of the student. We will study the major trends, the wide sweep of the emerging human consciousness, demanding—as it ceaselessly does—a change in education, religion and social organisation commensurate with its unfoldment. Civilisations, cultures, races and nations appear and disappear, but the same *individualities* come and go with them, garnering the fruits of experience, and progressively marching on to fuller *Self*-government and group organisation and synthesis.

I would remind you also that there is a peculiar quality in every human being—an innate, inherent characteristic which is inevitably present—to which one might give the name of "mystical perception." I use this term in a far wider sense than is usually the case, and would have you regard this quality of mystical perception as inclusive of:

1. The mystical vision of the soul, of God and the universe.
2. The power to contact and appreciate the world of meaning, the subjective world of the emerging reality.
3. The power to love and to go out to that which is other than the self.
4. The capacity to grasp and to intuit ideas.
5. The ability to sense the unknown, the desirable and the desired. The consequent determination and persistence which enable man to seek, search for and demand that unknown reality. It is the mystical tendency which has produced the great mystics of world renown, the large number of explorers, discoverers and inventors.
6. The power to sense, register and record the good, the beautiful and the true. It is this that has produced the writer, the poet, the artist and the architect.
7. The urge to discover and to penetrate to the secrets of God and of nature. It is this which produced the scientist, and the religious man.

From a study of these definitions you will see how inclusive the term "mystical perception" is. It is no more and
no less than the power, innate in man, to reach out and
to grasp that which is greater and better than himself,
and which has driven him on, through progressively developing cultures and civilisations, until today he stands on the
verge of a new kingdom in nature. It is the power to appreciate and to strive after the apparently unattainable
good. Let this broad and general thesis therefore be in
your minds as we study man's developing power of self-
expression, self-determination and self-government.

What are the basic ideas (beginning with the recognised
instincts) which have led man, step by step, to his present
struggle for world betterment, group evaluation and natural
self-determination, with a view—unconscious for the most
part—of providing a better organ of expression within the
living organism, humanity?

I dealt with this elsewhere when discussing the present
Ray Plan for humanity in the field of politics, of religion and
of education, and I should like to repeat part of what is there
said for it has a direct bearing on our theme:

"In the final analysis, the main problem of world government is the wise use of ideas. It is here that the power of
speech makes itself felt, just as in the department of religion or of education the power of the written word, of the
printed page, is felt. In the field of politics, the masses are
swayed by their orators, and never more so than now through
the use of the radio. Great ideas are dinned into the ear of
the public without cessation—theories as to dictatorship,
communism, nazism, fascism, marxism, nationalism and
democratic ideals. Methods of rule by this or that group
of thinkers are presented to the public, leaving them no
time for consideration, or for clear thinking. Racial antipa-
thies are spread, and personal preferences and illusions find
expression, bringing about the deception of the unthinking.

The man who has a golden tongue, the man who has the gift of playing with words and can voice with emphasis people's grievances, the juggler in statistics, the fanatic with a certain and sure cure for social ills and the man who loves to fan race hatreds, can ever get a following. Such men can with facility upset the balance of the community and lead a body of unthinking adherents to a transient success and power, or to obloquy and oblivion.

"In the aggregate of this play with ideas, and in the constant impact upon the human consciousness of the great concepts which lie back of our evolutionary process, the race is developing the power to think, to choose, and to build a sure foundation. Through the evolutionary presentation of these ideas there is a steady march towards a liberty of thought (through the old method of experiment, of discard, and of renewed effort with ever newer concepts) which will enable mankind to build true to the great thought patterns which underlie the outer structure of our world. The attentive minds of the age are constantly being made sensitive to these patterns, so that the individual mind can recognise them and wrest them out of the darkness into the light of day. Thus will the true patterns be made available, to play their part in leading the race towards its destiny, towards those deeper realisations which mould the racial types, and to that synthesis of understanding which will result in a realisation of Brotherhood. Thus thoughts play their part, and the problem of ideas will be increasingly understood, until the time may come when we shall have our trained intuitives and thinkers who will be able to work directly in the world of concepts and bring through (for the use of the race) the pattern ideas upon which to build. In saying this I realise that I may be accused of romancing and of communicating the impossible; but time will demonstrate the truth of that which I predict. The world structure emerges from and is built upon certain inner thought patterns, and it is these thought patterns which are producing the present flood of governmental experiments among all nations. But today there is no training given upon the process of contacting the world of patterns and upon the true interpretation of ideas, and hence the problems. Later, when the race sees its problem with clarity, it will act with wisdom and train with care its Observers and Communicators. These will be men and women in whom the intuition has awakened at the behest of an urgent intellect; they will be people whose minds are so subordinated to the group good, and so free from all sense of separativeness, that their minds present no impediment to the contact with the world of reality and of inner truth. They will not necessarily be people who could be termed 'religious' in the ordinary sense of that word, but they will be men of goodwill, of high mental calibre, with minds well stocked and equipped; they will be free from personal ambition and selfishness, animated by love of humanity and by a desire to help the race. Such a man is a spiritual man."

A Treatise on the Seven Rays, Vol. I, p. 179-181.

REASONS FOR THE PRESENT WORLD UNREST

Let me list for you some of the reasons for the present world unrest, reminding you that many of them are based upon causes which lie in so remote a past that history knows nothing of them, and they appear meaningless to you because you have no clear idea of the nature of early humanity. Some grasp of the essential situation will be of value if you are to follow development in the future intelligently.

First, *the point reached by humanity* itself is one of the major and primary causes. This evolutionary status has brought mankind to the threshold of a door upon the great path of evolution and has indicated an unfoldment which necessitates drastic changes in man's entire attitude to life and to all his world relations. These changes are being self-initiated by him and are not imposed upon him by an outside force or by the coercion of humanity in any form. This is an important point to be grasped. It might therefore be stated that:

1. Man is now at the point where the principle of intelligence is so strongly awakened within him that nothing can arrest his progress into knowledges which would be dangerously misused and selfishly applied if nothing were done to call a halt and thus safeguard him from himself—even at the cost of temporary pain. He must be taught to react to a higher and better sense of values.

2. Millions of human beings are now integrated or at the point of integration. They are beginning to function as a unity within themselves, preparatory to a higher process which will enable them consciously to integrate into the greater Whole. From the form side of manifestation, mind, emotion and brain are working in unison. Now the higher correspondence of these lower forces—wisdom, love and direction—must appear; the more subtle energies must be enabled to express themselves. Instinctively and mystically, humanity perceives that need with a clear definiteness. The instinct to go forward to higher achievement, to enquire and to search for that which is better, remains potent. Humanity can be trusted to push onward and to make progress. The Hierarchy of Love is, however, endeavouring to hasten the process, thereby taking the risk of complications in so doing.

3. Certain men and women in every field of human thought are expressing the potency of the unfoldment of their achieved integration and (if you will but believe it) the reality of their soul contact, by emerging out of the dead level of humanity. They stand forth above their fellows through the very force of their personality-integration and because they can

function as high grade and idealistic persons. From the altitude at which they stand (relatively high from the human standpoint, and interesting from the hierarchical point of view), they are seeking to mould the racial thought and life to a certain pattern which seems to them—according to their inclination, type and ray—to be desirable.

These individuals in the fields of government, religion, science, philosophy, economics and sociology are having a united powerful effect, some of it of a high and good order, some of it not so good. They affect their civilisation *materially* if their emphasis is there; they produce a cultural effect *subjectively* and *spiritually* if that is the impression they seek. Their motives are often sound and good, for they all have a touch of true idealism, but—being as yet inexperienced in the ways of the soul—they make many mistakes, are sidetracked in dangerous ways and lead many people into error and trouble. In the long run, the result will be the awakening of the public consciousness, and that is ever good.

Second, *the emerging of a new racial type*. The subjective outlines of this type can already clearly be seen. So glamoured are we by the form side that many claims are made today that the new race is to be found in America. The new race is forming in every land, but primarily in those lands where the fifth or Caucasian races are to be found. Among the fourth race peoples, however, a few, such as those to be found among the Chinese and the Japanese, are being discovered by the Hierarchy and are making their real and esoteric contribution to the whole.

Let me also make one definite statement at this point which may cause some surprise. The fifth kingdom in nature, the spiritual, will emerge out of the fifth root race. Such is the esoteric control of the Law of Correspondence. I would remind you nevertheless that the only fourth root race people to be found upon our planet are the Chinese, the Japanese, the various Mongoloid races in Central Asia (and they are somewhat intermixed with the Caucasian race) and the hybrid groups found in the many islands in the southern waters in both oceans and hemispheres, as well as the descendants of the races which a million years ago made the South American continent famous for its civilisation. I am necessarily widely generalising.

The new racial type is far more *a state of consciousness* than a physical form; it is a state of mind more than a peculiarly designed body. In time, however, any developed state of consciousness invariably conditions and determines the body nature and produces finally certain physical characteristics. The outstanding type of awareness of the coming new race will be the widespread recognition of the fact of the mystical perception. Its primary quality will be the intuitive understanding and control of energy; its contribution to the development of humanity is the transmutation of selfish desire into group love. This can be seen working out noticeably even today in the attitudes of great national leaders who are not, as a rule, animated at all by selfish ambition, but are controlled by love of their nation and thus by some definite form of idealism—hence the great emerging ideologies. Ponder on this point, get a wider picture of the growth of the human consciousness, and grasp somewhat the goal of the new and coming educational system.

Third, *the ending of the Piscean Age,* which has brought to the point of crystallisation (and therefore of death) all those forms through which the Piscean ideals have been moulded. They have served their purpose and done a great and needed work. It might be asked here: What are the major Piscean ideals?

1. *The idea of authority.* This has led to the imposition of the different forms of paternalism upon the

race—political, educational, social and religious paternalism. This may be either the kindly paternalism of the privileged classes, seeking to ameliorate the condition of their dependents (and there has been much of this) ; or the paternalism of the churches, the religions of the world, expressing itself as ecclesiastical authority; or the paternalism of an educational process.

2. *The idea of the value of sorrow and of pain.* In the process of teaching the race the necessary quality of *detachment,* in order that its desire and plans shall no longer be oriented to form living, the Guides of the race have emphasised the idea of the virtues of sorrow and the educational value of pain. These virtues are real, but the emphasis has been overdone by the lesser teachers of the race, so that the racial attitude today is one of sorrowful and fearful expectancy and a feeble hope that some reward (in a desirable and usually material form, such as the heaven of the various world religions) may eventuate after death, and thus compensate for all that has been undergone during life. The races today are steeped in misery and an unhappy psychological acquiescence in sorrow and pain. The clear light of love must sweep away all this and joy will be the keynote of the coming new age.

3. To the above thought must be coupled *the idea of self-sacrifice.* This idea has lately shifted from the individual and his sacrifice to the group presentation. The good of the whole is now held theoretically to be of such paramount importance that the group must gladly sacrifice the individual or group of individuals. Such idealists are apt to forget that the only true sacrifice is that which is self-initiated, and that when it is an enforced sacrifice (imposed by the more powerful and superior person or group) it is apt

to be, in the last analysis, the coercion of the individual and his enforced submission to a stronger will.

4. *The idea of the satisfaction of desire.* Above everything else, the Piscean Age has been the age of material production and of commercial expansion, of the
salesmanship of the products of human skill which
the general public is educated to believe are essential
to happiness. The old simplicity and the true values
have been temporarily relegated to the background.
This was permitted to continue without arrest for a
long period of time because the Hierarchy of Wisdom
sought to bring the people to the point of satiety.
The world situation is eloquent today of the fact
that possession and the multiplication of material
goods constitute a handicap and are no indications
that humanity has found the true road to happiness.
The lesson is being learnt very rapidly and the revolt
in the direction of simplicity is also rapidly gaining
ground. The spirit of which commercialism is the
indication is doomed, though not yet ended. This
spirit of possession and the aggressive taking of that
which is desired has proven widely inclusive and distinguishes the attitude of nations and of races as well
as individuals. Aggression in order to possess has
been the keynote of our civilisation during the past
fifteen hundred years.

Fourth, *the coming into manifestation of the Aquarian
Age.* This fact should provide the grounds for a profound
and convinced optimism; nothing can stop the effect—growing, stabilising and final—of the new, incoming influences.
These will inevitably condition the future, determine the
type of culture and civilisation, indicate the form of government and produce an effect upon humanity, as has the Piscean
or Christian Age, or the earlier period governed by Aries,
the Ram or Goat. Upon these steadily emerging influences

the Hierarchy counts with assurance, and the disciples of the world must likewise learn to depend upon them. The consciousness of universal relationship, of subjective integration and of a proven and experienced unity will be the climaxing gift of the period ahead of us.

In the coming world state, the individual citizen—gladly and deliberately and with full consciousness of all that he is doing—will subordinate his personality to the good of the whole. The growth of organised brotherhoods and fraternities, of parties and of groups, dedicated to some cause or idea, is another indication of the activity of the coming forces. The interesting thing to note is that they are all expressive of some grasped idea more than of some specific person's determined and imposed plan. The Piscean type of man is an idealist along some line of human development. The Aquarian type will take the new ideals and the emerging ideas and—in group activity—materialise them. It is with this concept that the education of the future will work. The idealism of the Piscean type and his life upon the physical plane were like two separate expressions of the man. They were often widely separated and were seldom fused and blended. The Aquarian man will bring into manifestation great ideals, because the channel of contact between soul and brain, via the mind, will be steadily established through right understanding, and the mind will be used increasingly in its dual activity—as the penetrator into the world of ideas and as the illuminator of life upon the physical plane. This will ultimately produce a synthesis of human endeavour and an expression of the truer values and of the spiritual realities such as the world has never yet seen. Such again is the goal of the education of the future.

What is the synthesis which will later be thus produced? Permit me to list a few factors without elaboration:

1. The fusion of man's differentiated spiritual aspirations, as expressed today in many world religions, into

the new world religion. This new religion will take the form of a conscious unified group approach to the world of spiritual values, evoking in its turn reciprocal action from Those Who are the citizens of that world —the planetary Hierarchy and affiliated groups.

2. The fusion of a vast number of men into various idealistic groups. These will form in every realm of human thought and they in turn will gradually be absorbed into ever larger syntheses. I would call your attention to the fact that if the various educational groups found in the world today, in every country, were to be listed, certain underlying and analogous trends would appear: their wide diversification, their basic foundation upon some idea of human betterment and their unity of goal. Their many ramifications and subsidiary groups constitute a vast interlocking network throughout the world which is indicative of two things:

    a. The steadily growing power of the man in the street to think in terms of ideals which are founded upon certain ideas and which have been put forward by some great intuitive.

    b. The gradual upward shift of man's aspirational consciousness by these ideas, his recognition of the idealism of his fellow men and his consequent training in the spirit of inclusiveness.

This growing trend towards idealism and inclusiveness is, in the last analysis, a trend towards love-wisdom. The fact that men today misapply these ideals, lower the vision and distort the true picture of the desired goal, and prostitute the early grasp of beauty to the satisfaction of selfish desire, should not prevent the realisation that the spirit of idealism is growing in the world and is not, as in the past, confined to a few advanced groups or one or two great intuitives. The discussions of the man in the street are today connected with some political, social, educational or religious philosophy, based on some school of idealism. From the standpoint of Those Who are responsible for man's evolutionary development, a great step forward has been made in the last two hundred years. What were the themes of the intellectuals and the philosophers in the middle ages are today the points for animated discussion in restaurants, railway carriages, or wherever people consort, argue and talk. This is apt to be forgotten, and I would ask you to ponder on its implications and to enquire what is liable to be the final outcome of this widespread ability of the human mind to think in terms of the larger Whole and not only in terms of personal interest, and to apply forms of idealistic philosophy to the life of practical affairs. Today man does both these things.

What, therefore, does this indicate? It signifies a trend in the consciousness of humanity towards the fusion of the individual with the whole, without his losing, at the same time, his sense of individuality. Whether he joins a political party, or upholds some form of welfare work, or joins some of the many groups occupied with forms of esoteric philosophy, or becomes a member of some prevalent ism or cult, he is increasingly aware of an expansion of consciousness and of a willingness to identify his personal interests with those of a group which has for its basic objective the materialising of some ideal. Through this process it is believed that the conditions of human living will be bettered or some need will be met.

This process is going on today in every nation and in all parts of the world, and a census of the world educational groups and the world religious groups (to mention only two out of many possible categories) would prove the staggering number of such bodies and affiliations. It would indicate the differentiation of thought, and at the same time substantiate my conclusion that men are everywhere turning towards synthesis, fusion, blending and mutual cooperation for certain visioned and specific ends. It is, for mankind, a new field of expression and of enterprise. Hence the frequent misapplications of the newer truths, the distortion of the values sensed and the perversion of the truth to suit individual aims and ends. But as man gropes his way along these lines, and as the many ideas and the various ideologies present to him points of choice and indicate emerging standards of living and of relationship, he will gradually learn to think with greater clarity, to recognise the differing aspects of truth as expressions of a basic subjective reality, and —relinquishing no part of the truth which has set him or his group free—he will learn also to include his brother's truth along with his own.

When this attitude has been developed in the field of practical education we shall find nations and individuals developing the ideas which seem to suit the national or personal psychology, yet recognising the reality, potency and usefulness of the point of view of other individuals and nations. When, for instance, the ideas contained in the teaching on the seven rays are of general recognition, we shall find the growth of psychological understanding, and the nations and the world religions will arrive at mutual understanding.

The Angle of Parenthood

I began with the angle of citizenship for two definite reasons: first, because it is a basic rule in esotericism to argue always from the universal to the particular, and secondly, the theme of citizenship, of the relationship of the unit to the whole and of the individual to the state, is the all-engrossing topic today in world affairs. With it newspapers, radio dialogues and governmental appeals all deal. This subject necessarily embodies the whole problem of individual freedom and of collective responsibility. This subtle relationship must be understood and expressed by humanity in line with the underlying principles of the entire human and planetary structure. This structure is that of an all-embracing Hierarchy. In spite of the rationalisation of men's minds, this Hierarchy exists and extends from the atom of substance at the very depth of manifestation to the entire solar system; it expresses in its graded ascent every type of consciousness, from that of the infinitesimally small to that of the infinitely great. It is with a small section of the hierarchical structure— and a very small section at that—that we are engaged. Our field of investigation is that of the fourth Creative Hierarchy, which is the hierarchy of human beings; it concerns the relations of the members of this hierarchy within its hierarchical periphery; it deals also with a possible range of existence in the subhuman realms on a lower rung of the ladder of hierarchical existence, and with that hierarchical structure which is found immediately above the human in the scale of being, that of the fifth or spiritual kingdom, the Kingdom of God.

With that great hierarchical unit which we call the animal kingdom, the third kingdom in nature, man is definitely related through the medium of his animal, etheric and astral bodies. He is also related to the kingdom of souls, because his own soul is an integral part of that kingdom, just as his physical body is an integral part of the animal kingdom. The aspect of himself which is strictly and specifically human is the mind or mental body; this is essentially the organ of relationship to all other human races.

In connection with our subject, therefore, I would have you bear in mind that the "threads of lighted consciousness" which we unfailingly create, and which eventually form the antahkarana, have to be woven between each and every hierarchical unit, and that within the human kingdom itself these connecting relationships and bridging factors have to be established between unit and unit and between group and group.

In the earlier stages this is effected on a mass scale by

means of the influence of the prevailing culture and civilisation. This, through its external impact and through the medium of its telepathic influence, makes a gradual and slow change, for at the beginning of the evolutionary process development is so slow as to be scarcely recognisable. Inevitably, however, subjective changes are wrought in the life of the individual. As evolution proceeds the process becomes increasingly rapid, until today in the so-called civilised countries, the areas affected by civilisation are speedily widening and the cultural effects are as rapidly deepening.

It is hard for the modern thinker to conceive of that time when there was no racial, national or blended religious consciousness such as is expressing itself in the world today. Even the most imaginative man is unable to visualise a state of mind wherein the consciousness was purely instinctive, self-engrossed in the physical sense, and unable to register any wider contacts than those of mate, offspring, and the call of physical appetites. Some study of such a state of consciousness has been attempted in connection with the evolution of the tribes which are fast dying out in the modern world, but even here it is impossible to make adequate allowance for the subtler impressions and influences which are the result of united thought and inner mental pressure of the civilised part of humanity. Gradually the world of men has become increasingly self-aware and is being sharply differentiated (with the relationship at the same time recognised) from the animal. The state of consciousness related to the kingdom of souls is divided into various psychological schools, or is termed either occult or mystical.

We could therefore, in connection with the consciousness of humanity, divide the entire subject into three parts:

1. That concerning the tangible apparatus, the animal body, and the response mechanism whereby objective and outer contacts are made possible.
2. That concerning the inner or psychological life of

man. This consists mainly of desire, aspiration, ambition and mental activity, and all of these can manifest either in their animal, psychical, mental or spiritual forms.
3. That concerning the spiritual life of man and his relationship to the world of souls, which involves, incidentally, his relationship to his own soul.

As time has progressed, these three developing aspects in
the realm of consciousness have brought humanity to the
recognition, not only of man's own inner personal relationships (incidentally leading to an understanding of his own
physical, psychological and mental equipment), but they
have brought mankind also to a realisation of the various
human group relationships of which the first and the most
important hitherto has been the family group-unit. It is
here that one of the major distinctions between the human
state of consciousness and that of the animal has developed,
through the divine imposition of the Law of Necessity. This
law has provided opportunity for the development of the
sense of responsibility for the care of the family. Once an
animal or a bird can fend for itself physically, it is cast off
by the parent or parents and left to its own resources. In
the case of the human family, the physical care of the child,
as well as its psychological unfoldment, has gradually been
extended until either the parent or the church, the community or the state, is responsible for him for many years—
the time element varying according to the country of birth
and social status.

This has entirely altered the aspect of affairs and the
first group, therefore, of which any individual child becomes
normally aware is the family group as a unit in the community. In that particular group relationship, throughout
the ages (both symbolically and indeed in fact), the following factors—underlying the very structure of existence itself—

are preserved and developed and are held before the race as that which is ultimately ideal:

1. *The recognition of hierarchical status,* which is, in the last analysis, the relation of the lesser to the greater, of the weaker to the stronger and of the more experienced to the less experienced. Thereby the sense of protection is developed, which is the working out of one form of the love aspect in the universe.

2. *The recognition of responsibility,* inherited, applied or shouldered. This is the relation of the older to the younger, of the wise to the ignorant. Thereby the need of providing opportunity for the unfoldment of knowledge is developed.

3. *The recognition of the faculty of forgiveness,* which is, or rather should be, the expression of the relationship between unit and unit within the larger group, or of group and group within a still larger whole. Forgiveness is essentially the process whereby each gives to each along psychical lines, and it is one of the rudimentary expressions of the quality of self-sacrifice which is, in its turn, an aspect of the will nature of Deity. Being therefore related to the monadic or will life, it is as yet completely misunderstood and misinterpreted. It is in reality the sense of synthesis or of identification and of "each for all and all for each." This sense is being developed today as never before, but it is still so embryonic that words do not help in explaining it. This faculty of forgiveness is not a form of magnanimous forgetting or overlooking, neither is it a gesture of superiority whereby the slate is wiped clean. It is the very breath of life itself—the giving of all to all and for all.

4. *The recognition of group interplay* within the larger world relationship—justly, harmoniously and rhyth-

mically. It is the sense of right relations, carried forward consciously and harmoniously developed.

In the period which is coming, and under the influence of the new education, these four basic recognitions will be inculcated and taught to every child in school and college. They will thus govern and develop the new form of family unit which must inevitably come into existence.

The family group (like all else in human affairs) has shared in the general separativeness, selfishness and individual, isolated exclusiveness, based on class distinctions, inherited tradition, racial attitudes and national custom. Families (under any category and bracket) present a united front to the world; parents defend their own children and position and situation, right or wrong; family pride, tradition, pedigree are overemphasised, leading to the different barriers which today separate man from man, family from family and group from group. The grip of the past upon families is a factor which is largely responsible for the revolt of modern youth against parental control, though other factors—such as rebellion against enforced religion and old outworn standards and philosophies—are equally responsible. However, under the coming world order, educators will prepare the young people in school and college for participation in an active and consciously realised group life. For this they will be prepared by training them in the recognition of the four factors I have listed as essential to human progress at this time. These will, when grasped and practiced, produce the needed right relationships and eventually a harmonious world.

Hierarchy, responsibility, group interplay, and forgiveness or sacrifice—these are the four categories of recognition which will enable each person to do his part and take his share in bridging between person and person, between group and group, and between nation and nation, thus establishing that new world of recognised corporate relationships which will eventually produce the civilisation of light and love which will be characteristic of the Aquarian Age.

It is these four concepts which lie behind the Science of the Antahkarana, the Science of Meditation, and the Science of Service. Their connotations have to be interpreted in no sentimental sense, or in the coin of current ideas, but always from the angle of a trained intelligence and of a spiritually developed consciousness.

Parenthood will not be regarded primarily as an animal function or as a purely social or economic function, which are the usual lines of approach at this present time. The establishing of a deliberately prepared or constructed thread of light (as a definite part of the world-antahkarana) between parent and child, even in the prenatal stages, will be carefully taught. Thus a close rapport will be brought about "in the light" yet without establishing undue mental control and authority. This latter sentence will show you how impossible it has been to date to hasten the teaching of this new science of the antahkarana. Today it is beginning to be possible to lay the foundation for this new teaching, because the young people in every land are forcing upon their parents and their teachers the idea of their essential and determined independence. The revolt of youth, in spite of all the immediate and individual disasters, has been a desirable thing and has prepared the way for the establishing of right and better relations, based upon the premises which I have laid down.

It is of course impossible for me to do more than indicate here the basis of the new education which will prepare the youth of the world for the responsibilities and duties of parenthood. The entire problem is tied up with that of sex, and also with the problem of the state and its control, far more than is generally conceded. Those are two problems which are only emerging today into their full significance, and with them I cannot here deal. Parenthood is the result, and the ordained result, of the relation of two animal bodies, and I would have you ponder—even if ineffectually—upon the wider group implications of this statement. Parenthood is what makes a state, a nation, and a group possible as far as manifestation is concerned, and here again the vastness of the problem is staggering. Parenthood has also a close symbolic relationship to the Hierarchy, for the family unit is the symbol upon earth of the Hierarchy, and it is through the two facts of sexual relationship and physical birth that the vast Hierarchy of Souls can achieve physical manifestation and attain spiritual perfection in the three worlds of human evolution. One could (and this fact should be carefully borne in mind) divide the Hierarchy into two basic groups:

1. Those souls who have reached perfection and achieved the status of divine servers.
2. Those souls who are in the processes of evolution and passing through the periods of continual incarnation.

The idea of generation, birth and subsequent manifestation runs like a guiding thread through all esoteric thought. The ancient teachers of the race, sent out by the Hierarchy from time to time, ever employed the symbolism of natural process in order to illustrate and make clear the needed instruction, and lay that spiritual foundation of truth which will in the coming age lead the race into new ways and a new manner of thought. For the esotericist, there is the process of birth into the darkness of physical incarnation which—in its turn—is the foreordained preparatory process which leads to birth into light, carried forward in the light and producing the externalisation of the body of light. This continuing process (for in all ages this birth into light has been going forward) will produce that future world of light which it is the purpose of the natural processes of evolution to reveal. This is the "second birth" spoken of in the New Testament, in which a man is "born again" into the world of light and love.

From the angle of the new education, these new concepts will govern the mental attitude of parents in the coming civilisation, and for this the adolescent must be prepared. It is the misinterpretation of the newer concepts which is prevalent at this time and is thus producing the emphasis laid—in certain countries and among nationalists of all countries—upon the necessity to increase the birth rate. Attention is now being paid to birth rate, its rise and fall, to correct care of mothers and children, even in the prenatal period, and to the education of parents everywhere. Out of all this, new ideas and attitudes must eventually arise which will be in line with the coming world culture and concepts. But today, the motive for this solicitude is wrong. The interior impulse to deal with the whole problem of parenthood in a newer and better way is right. The objectives, however, which are held before the race are not the highest or the most desirable. The necessity of the times will eventually produce radical changes in the approach to family life, parenthood and the training of children, and for this a nucleus is preparing the way—or can do so if faithful, attentive and intelligent work is done.

Trends Indicative of Future Developments

As I said before, this subject of parenthood and child training is too great for ample or satisfactory discussion in these brief instructions, but certain statements can be made which will be indicative of future developments and point the way to where the changed attitude may be anticipated. Let me list them as follows:

1. The emphasis in the future will shift from the urge to produce large families to that of producing *quality* and *intelligence* in the offspring.. This will include that science of which eugenics is the distorted and

exoteric indication. When the fact of the etheric body with its force centres is scientifically established, the above prophecy will assume significance and meaning.

2. The need of an increasing birthrate will be eventually regarded as erroneous, and this for three reasons which it would profit you to study:

a. Many souls are rapidly achieving perfection and passing away altogether from our planetary life. This process will be intensified during the coming Aquarian Age. It should be remembered that the door will be shut for some time as yet upon the animal kingdom, and for a long period no individualisation will culminate in materialisation into physical bodies. Technically, any individualisation which may take place will be that which is technically called "individualisation into pralaya, there to await the inevitable call." There will be, therefore, no necessity for a massed and hurried creation of human forms.

b. The economic situation will make it necessary that certain physical restrictions should be imposed, because it is now evident that *beyond a certain point the planet cannot support humanity.* This is more fundamental in its implications than you can imagine. Again, we have evidence of a growing realisation of the race along this particular line; that realisation is as yet distorted and much misunderstood and is today producing the promiscuous use of contraceptive methods. As the intelligence of the race is developed (and that is going on apace) , as the Laws of Rhythm and Approach are grasped, it will then be found that there are certain innate reactions which will negate conception, and that then the mechanical means will no longer be required. This sounds as yet extremely vague and almost impossible, but the race is rapidly achieving personality control (e'en though our idea of rapidity may not be yours) and this, in its turn, must produce certain automatic and inherent changes. This is a point which must be grasped by esotericists.

c. The widespread promiscuity of the sexes, and the rule in many countries which entitles a man to possess many wives (which is an insult to the woman), will eventually and inevitably cease. It is, in the last analysis, a form of legalised prostitution, and the fact that it has the endorsement of tradition and centuries of practice does not mitigate this position which I take. Through this lack of regulation and of essential rhythm, the natural consequences have occurred, and millions of souls have been brought into incarnation who were never intended *at this time* to incarnate and achieve exoteric manifestation. This fact is largely responsible for much of the present economic distress and for the modern planetary dilemma. The economic situation and the necessity to provide for the unduly large population of the planet lies behind much of the aggression and greed of the nations down the ages, and for the effort being made today as never before to provide better and more adequate living conditions. War has consequently been the inevitable result of this undue and unlimited propagation of the human species. This lack of sexual control has brought into the world thousands of unwanted children whose appearance is solely the result of accidental and uncontrolled sexual relations, and in no way indicates the planned intention of parents— planned because intended to offer experience to incarnating souls, with the conscious intent of offering the opportunity to hasten the "birth into the light" of those particular souls, thus rendering service to the divine plan.

3. The science of eugenics and of sex hygiene and the development of mentally controlled relationships will steadily grow. Much that is now taught along these lines is erroneous and wrongly motivated, being based upon fear, expediency and the desire for improved racial attributes and physical perfection. The right form of scientific sex control, leading to those right conditions in which souls may incarnate, cannot be imposed by law. The desired ends may be aided by educational methods and already this is being done in a tentative and embryonic manner; but the real change in human consciousness which is needed will appear only as the race itself is brought under a rhythmic law—under which, for instance, the animal lives function, or the seasonal law under which forms in the vegetable kingdom operate—thus transferring the whole concept on to a higher turn of the evolutionary spiral. This, when it is brought about, will produce certain fundamental changes—regulated sex life, an organised parental life, and mental differences in the racial attitude towards the sex relation and its ordained consequence, *Birth*.

4. As yet, it is only the religious person who thinks in terms of the two necessitated and inevitable births, the physical and the spiritual, and he thinks of the relation between the two as purely symbolic and not in any way to be interpreted literally. Yet there is a close relation and an analogy between the two which, as time elapses, will become more clear. There can be no new birth, no creation of the "body of light," and no "manifestation of the sons of God" apart from the process of physical incarnation. There can be no fusion of the opposites of soul and personality

apart from the physiological processes of sex, and
I say this deliberately, for it is in the relation of the
sexes that the element of time enters into the experience of the soul, and the understanding of this will
come when the doctrine of reincarnation is properly
comprehended and taught universally. It is here that
sex magic and the inner tantric teachings have gone
so woefully astray, and been centralised upon individual development and the attainment of some experience which is presumed to promote spiritual attainment. The underlying idea, governing all that
has been given out on the sex relation heretofore, is
twofold in its implications:

a. To provide bodies for incarnating souls so that
    certain destined evolutionary unfoldments may be
    carried forward, and the attainment of an equally
    destined and inevitable spiritual unfoldment be-
    comes possible.

b. To impart the scientific procedure whereby bodies
    "built in the dark" may gradually be superseded
    by bodies "built in the light." Thus will be
    brought about the manifestation of the founda-
    tional *light aspect* of the world and its underlying
    structure.

5. The sex relation has, therefore, only one major ob-
    jective, which is to produce physical bodies for incar-
    nating souls. The relation between the soul and the
    personality is consequently a higher aspect of the
    basic sex expression of the universe, and this rela-
    tion is intended to bring about the appearance of a
    son of God as light in the world, enabling him to
    say, as did the Christ, that he is "the light of the
    world," and to fulfill the injunction, "let your light
    shine." Again, the relation between humanity and
    the Hierarchy is intended to produce the radiance of
    group light and cause to emerge, out of these two

planetary groups or bodies, through their close fusion
and scientific interrelation, that form of divine manifestation to which the name "the Kingdom of God"
has been given in the West.

I would ask you to ponder on these five points or statements which are only intended to be suggestive, to evoke
brooding thought and to indicate those elementary ideas
which will bring in the newer attitudes to parental responsibility. In the world today there are many thinking men
and women who are conscious of and earnestly desiring the
above, and who are working towards these ends. But the
mass of the people in their untold millions are totally un-
aware of the situation, either in its economic or esoteric
aspects. One of the tasks of the educator of the future will
be to teach the meaning of the Law of Rebirth, and thus
bring about such a profound change in the racial attitude to
life and sex, to birth and parenthood, that sex rhythm, cyclic
experience, psychological preparation and directed, controlled body-building may go forward and supersede the
present methods, which are based upon an uncontrolled
response to the sex urge and desire, and the unthinking
procreation of children. The vast population of the world
today is the result of an animal response to those urges and
of the general promiscuity, which is perhaps the outstanding
factor, esoterically speaking and from the standpoint of the
Hierarchy, of the present world distress, economic difficulties and national aggressions. Think this out, for it holds
a clue.

Summing up very briefly, I would say that the objective
before the race as it enters into the new age is to "create in
the light through the ordained activity of the light-body."
This involves the understanding of the different light expressions—the light of understanding, the light of a pre-
arranged and comprehended process and the light of experience. With these more subtle aspects of light leading,

controlling and directing the human consciousness in relation to racial generation and the perpetuation of the species, and with the science of light (a science dealing with that which concerns substance and form, for it must not be forgotten that light and substance are synonymous terms) forming an integral part of the education of parents and adolescents, we can then look forward to adjustments and changes, which are bound to come, with confidence and assurance that all will be well.

The motives leading to marriage will undergo profound changes during the next one thousand years, though the basic motive—that of love between two people—will remain unchanged or more properly emphasised and selflessly expressed. The attitude of parents towards their children will alter drastically and the responsibility angle will be continuously emphasised, though that responsibility will be concerned primarily with the time, opportunity and correctness of producing the forms which incarnating souls will assume. The idea of the need for rapid procreation and the production of large families through which the state can achieve its end will be changed. The preparation of adults for the duties of parenthood and their training in the basic necessities of the coming child will shift increasingly to the mental and spiritual levels of consciousness and be less given to physical preparations. The light which is in the parents, which in the days to come will be seen clairvoyantly by an increasing number of people, will be scientifically related to the embryonic light in the child, and the thread of light connecting parent and child (of which the umbilical cord is the exoteric symbol) will be skillfully and patiently constructed. The child will come into incarnation with its light body already embedded and functioning in the physical body and this will be due to the intelligent mental work of the parents. This is not so today, except in the case of very advanced egos, for the light body is inchoate and diffused and simply hovers over the physical form of the child, waiting for an opportunity to enter and irradiate the consciousness. Thus will be brought about an integration in the light substance of the planet which is lacking at this time; and the production of this integration will be definitely initiated by the trained parents of the new age and facilitated, as the child matures, by the teaching and influence of the illumined educator.

This all sounds to you necessarily peculiar and too abstract and farfetched to make much sense. I would have you remember that much which is familiar to you today and which constitutes a definite part of the recognised facts of daily life would, a few hundred years ago, have been regarded as equally peculiar, incomprehensible and impossible. What is really taking place is the hastening of the processes of light manifestation, and this has become possible because of the point of attainment of humanity and the increased stimulation which is being applied to the race by the Hierarchy, assisted by forces emanating from Shamballa.

THE ANGLE OF PERSONALITY CONTROL

Much that I could say here would simply be a repetition of that which you already know and have been taught. Many of you who are reading my words here are steeped in the ideas which I have been seeking to impart to humanity for the past years, for it was in 1919 that I first started writing through the cooperation of A.A.B. In these writings I have sought to do two things:

1. Teach the basic necessity for certain great fusions—individual, racial and spiritual:

    a. The fusion or integration of the different aspects of man's nature—physical, emotional and mental. When this has been accomplished we shall have the manifestation of the integrated elemental forces to which we give the name of the Personality, producing the manifestation of a powerful, self-directed, high grade human being.

b. The fusion of the personality and the soul. This has to be carried out consciously and deliberately, with the willingness of these related parts of a great divine whole to see the personality subjected to changes and transmutations, produced as a result of soul contact. This will lead to the manifestation of the indwelling soul, the Christ consciousness, the Solar Angel.

c. The ultimate fusion of humanity with the Hierarchy, producing the manifestation of God's Kingdom on earth. This will be the consummation of all the other fusions, and will have produced certain great planetary, racial and national fusions which are incidental and necessary to progress and its inevitable results.

These fusions are not carried forward as listed above in an ordered sequential fashion. There is much overlapping and lack of balance in the process, but though there may be differences and difficulties in the lengthy process, the end is inevitable and unalterable. The Kingdom of God, the consummation of it all, will appear upon the planet.

2. Inculcate the methods, productive of quality and not just of quantity, which will facilitate the emergence of certain great divine characteristics. These will, in due time, change the world and bring in the new attitudes and states of consciousness. These, when they are matured and recognised, will bring about the appearance of the culture and civilisation which is, for the race, the next planned and desired development.

Need I, therefore, talk to you about personality development and control? Is not that something which you have

considered and worked at for years? Can I tell you anything of a practical nature that you do not already know
and strive to attain? Shall I increase your present responsibility by repetition? I think not. The new culture will
emerge and come into being, as all of those who have a
consciousness of light and the goal of pure service (which
such a consciousness inevitably entails) proceed with their
appointed task—a self-appointed task in every case—of living
and teaching the truth about light, as opportunity offers.

CHAPTER V

The Science of the Antahkarana

A S A PREPARATION for what students need to master, I would like to emphasise certain points by tabulating the information already given. The Science of the Antahkarana is not an easy one to learn because of the following points. These emphasised points must be accepted by students as a working hypothesis prior to all attempted work:

1. The Science of the Antahkarana is connected with the entire problem of energy, but peculiarly with the energy handled by the individual and with the forces by which the individual relates himself to other individuals or to groups. For the sake of clarity, we will give the name of

    a. ENERGY: to all forces pouring into the individual form from whatever direction and source. To these major energies, the names of "sutratma" or "life thread" or "silver cord" have frequently been given.

    b. FORCE: to all the energies which—after due manipulation and concentration—are projected by the individual or group in any direction and with many possible motives, some good and many selfish.

2. The Science of the Antahkarana, technically speaking and for group purpose, is especially the science of

light manifestation with its results of revelation and consequent changes. It should be remembered that:

a. Light is substantial, and from the angle of the spirit is a sublimation or higher form of material matter.

b. Light is also the quality or major characteristic of the soul in its own realm, and of the etheric body (a reflection of the soul eventually) in the three worlds of human evolution.

c. The object of the science with which we are dealing is to fuse the lower and the upper lights, so that one light shines forth in physical manifestation and a synthesis of light is consequently brought about.

d. Technically speaking, two light bodies exist—the vital or etheric body and the soul vehicle. One is the result of aeons of incarnating life and becomes in time a powerful repository of energies gathered out of a wide range of contacts, though conditioned by the ray type in its three aspects. The etheric body exists and is today functioning powerfully. The soul body is in process of being slowly constructed, and is that "house not made with hands, eternal in the heavens" to which the New Testament refers (II Cor. 5:1). It is interesting to note that the Old Testament refers to the etheric body (Ecc. 12:6-7) and its construction, and the New Testament deals with the building of the spiritual body.

3. The Science of the Antahkarana must be studied in three ways:

a. *Concretely* and in relation to the etheric body, which is a substantial, tangible form, and is being so considered (though not as yet universally admitted) by modern science.

b. *Egoically* and in relation to the soul and to the "light body" through which the spiritual man must function in the world of souls, and which—when blended and fused with the etheric body—produces the manifestation of divinity upon earth to a greater or lesser degree, according to the extent of fusion and *the conscious recognition by the individual* of the attained fusion.

c. *Abstractly* and in relation to knowledge-wisdom, which are two words used in relation to force and energy, and their use by the individual in his environment and contacts. Ponder on these words. You will realise how necessary it is that there should be some capacity for abstract thinking before the true implications of this new science can be understood.

4. The Science of the Antahkarana is concerned with the problem of the continuity of consciousness and with the problem of life and death. Keep these two themes clearly in your mind for they are basic and important.

5. The Science of the Antahkarana deals with the three-fold thread which connects:

a. The monad, the soul and the personality, linking all three periodical vehicles and unifying all seven principles.

b. The triple personality and its environment in the three worlds of human enterprise, and later in the other two worlds (making five) of super-human expression.

c. The consciously creative man and the world of ideas. These he must contact and express through creative work, thus bridging with the light:

1. Between the world of souls and the world of phenomena.

2. Between the realm of subjective beauty and reality and the outer tangible world of nature.
3. Between himself and others.
4. Between group and group.
5. Later, when the divine Plan has become a reality to him, between the fourth kingdom (the human) and the fifth kingdom (the Kingdom of God).
6. Finally, between humanity and the Hierarchy.

6. The Science of the Antahkarana is the science of the triple thread which exists from the very beginning of time and links individual man with his monadic source. The recognition of this thread and its use, consciously, as the Path and the means of ever expanding contacts, comes relatively late in the evolutionary process. The goal of all aspirants and disciples is to become aware of this stream of energy in its various diversifications and consciously to employ these energies in two ways: interiorly in self-unfoldment, and in the service of the plan for humanity.

7. The Science of the Antahkarana teaches certain fundamental truths about the thread, some of which might be enumerated as follows:

   a. The *life thread* comes directly from the monad or the ONE. This thread is anchored in the heart during incarnation. There is the seat of life.
   b. The *consciousness thread* comes directly from the soul. It is anchored in the head. There is the seat of consciousness.
   c. The *thread of creative activity* is initiated and constructed by the human being. It is anchored, when sufficiently constructed, in the throat. This thread is an extension or synthesis of the two basic threads.

The creative thread itself is triple in nature. It is slowly constructed down the ages by the man. As he becomes truly alive, from the standpoint of intelligent awareness and the desire fully to express himself, the process is materially hastened. These three self-created lesser threads which constitute the third thread of the antahkarana extend eventually:

1. From the physical body to the etheric body, passing from the heart to the spleen, and thence to the body of prana, the vital or etheric body, *unites with force from the egoic will petals.*
2. From the etheric body to the astral body. This thread passes from the solar plexus to the heart and from thence to the astral body, picking up the energy of the thread mentioned above, *unites with force from the love petals.*
3. From the astral body to the mental vehicle. This thread passes from the ajna centre to the head centre and from thence to the mind body, picking up the energy of the other two threads mentioned above, *unites with the force from the knowledge petals.*

Though these three energies are woven into one thread finally, yet they remain distinct. It should be borne in mind that the soul body is constructed of pure white light,whilst the light out of which the etheric body is made is golden.

8. The Science of the Antahkarana deals, therefore, with the entire incoming system of energy, with the processes of usage and transformation and fusion. It deals also with the outgoing energies and their relationship to the environment and is the basis of

the science of the force centres. The incoming an'
the outgoing energies constitute finally two great
stations of energy, one characterised by power and
the other by love, and all directed to the illumination of the individual and of humanity as a whole,
through the medium of the Hierarchy composed of
individuals. This is basically the Science of the
Path.

The antahkarana, therefore, is the thread of *consciousness,* of intelligence, and the responsive agent in all
sentient reactions. The interesting point to bear in mind,
and where we must now lay the emphasis, is that this thread
of consciousness *is evolved by the soul* and not by the monad.
The World Soul pours its gossamer thread of sentient consciousness into all forms, into all body cells and into all
atoms. The human soul, the solar angel, repeats the process
in relation to its shadow and reflection, the personality.
This is part of the creative work of the soul. But, in its
turn, the human being has also to become creative in the
mental sense of the term and must repeat the process, for
in all points the microcosm resembles the macrocosm.
Therefore, through the life thread, the soul creates and
reproduces a personality through which to function. Then
through the building of the antahkarana, the soul first of
all develops sentiency down upon the physical plane, and
later bridges the gap—through meditation and service—
between the three mental aspects. It thus completes the
creation of the path of return to the Centre, which must
parallel the path of outgoing.

I have now completed my introductory presentation of
the fundamentals which will in the future age dominate the
educational systems. It was necessary for all of you—and for
those who will later study these instructions anent the new
education—to have some grasp of past foundational implications and basic tendencies and also some ideas, however

vague, of the line along which major changes can be expected to come. You can begin, therefore, to work intelligently and with as little loss of time as possible.

It remains now to make the teaching which I have given practical in its implications. The New Education now must take the place of that which is old and which has proved so wrong that it could not prevent the universal holocaust which distinguished the years 1914-1945. It must be superseded. The next stage of human evolution will emerge as a result of the purificatory action of the World War. There are steps which humanity must take, and only a new type of education and a different attitude to the educational processes (imposed upon the very young of every nation) will enable mankind to take them.

A new cycle of experience, of psychological development and of new educational processes is imminent. What I have given here and elsewhere on the Science of Meditation, of Service and anent the Antahkarana gives method, mode, promise and point to it all.

THE TIBETAN

THE GREAT INVOCATION

From the point of Light within the Mind of God
  Let light stream forth into the minds of men.
    Let Light descend on Earth.

From the point of Love within the Heart of God
  Let love stream forth into the hearts of men.
    May Christ return to Earth.

From the centre where the Will of God is known
  Let purpose guide the little wills of men —
    The purpose which the Masters know and serve.

From the centre which we call the race of men
  Let the Plan of Love and Light work out
    And may it seal the door where evil dwells.

Let Light and Love and Power restore the Plan on Earth.

"The above Invocation or Prayer does not belong to any person or group but to all humanity. The beauty and the strength of this Invocation lies in its simplicity, and in its expression of certain central truths which all men, innately and normally, accept — the truth of the existence of a basic Intelligence to Whom we vaguely give the name of God; the truth that behind all outer seeming, the motivating power of the universe is Love; the truth that a great Individuality came to earth, called by Christians, the Christ, and embodied that love so that we could understand; the truth that both love and intelligence are effects of what is called the Will of God; and finally the self-evident truth that only through *humanity* itself can the Divine Plan work out."

ALICE A. BAILEY

SYNOPSIS

The following synopsis in three sections is intended to give the student a comprehensive grasp of the ideas upon which the teaching of the New Education is based. It is not a table of contents but gives some insight into the nature of the results to be obtained. Section One is developed in this book and lays the foundation for Section Two which appears in *A Treatise on the Seven Rays, Vol. V*, constituting part of more advanced teaching. Section Three completes the thesis by adding the Science of Service which is the goal of the whole enterprise.

EDUCATION IN THE NEW AGE

Section One: The Objectives of the Future Education

  I. The Cultural Unfoldment of the Race.
 II. The Next Step in the Mental Development of the Race.
    A. In the present transition period.
    B. In the Aquarian Age.
III. The Culture of the Individual in order to make him:
    A. An intelligent citizen of two worlds.
    B. A wise parent.
    C. A controlled and directed personality.

Section Two: The Antahkarana

  I. The Nature of the Antahkarana.
    A. The bridge between the three aspects of the mind:
      1. The lower concrete mind, the receptive common sense.
      2. The individualised mind or the soul, the spiritual ego.
      3. The higher abstract mind or the factor of the intuition.
    B. The agent of alignment between:
      1. Mind and brain or man in the three worlds.
      2. Personality and soul.

II. The Technique of Constructing the Antahkarana.
  A. Its construction up till the present time.
  B. The immediate task ahead.
  C. The seven ray methods employed in this construction process.

III. The Antahkarana and the New Education.
  A. The practical results of the new technique:
    1. Will induce wholeness or the ability to see life whole.
    2. Will foster the sense of synthesis and therefore the group spirit.
    3. Will develop the intuition and the ability to contact the world of ideas.
    4. Will train the will, especially the will-to-good.
  B. The mystical results will be:
    1. The development of the mystical sense and the mystical realisation of duality.
    2. The recognition of a new objective:
      a. The objective is to integrate the personality.
      b. Next, the objective is to give the vision of the soul, the central self.
  C. The occult results will be:
    1. The bringing about of the at-one-ment or the identification of the personality with the central self, the soul.
    2. The mind, then, will be trained and become an intermediary between soul and personality.

Section Three: The Three Major Sciences of the Aquarian Age

I. The Science of the Antahkarana.
  A. The mystical realisation of duality.
    1. The problem of the integrated personality.
    2. The vision of the soul, the central self.
    3. The problem of the mystic.
  B. Occult identification or at-one-ment.
    1. The integration of soul and personality.
    2. The mind as an intermediary.
    3. The problem of equilibrium or steadiness.

C. The application of these concepts to the immediate educational necessity.

II. The Science of Meditation.
  A. Meditation as an education technique.
    1. Right control of the mind.
    2. The two functions of the mind.
    3. The mind as it builds the antahkarana.
  B. Meditation in the world of ideas.
    1. The power to intuit.
    2. Sensitivity and response to higher impressions.
    3. The function and promulgation of ideas.
  C. The development of continuity of consciousness.
    1. Personality continuity.
    2. Continuity and immortality.
    3. Continuity and initiation.

III. The Science of Service.
  A. Service as a result of soul contact.
  B. Service as cooperation with the plan.
  C. Service as a technique of group development.
  D. The unfoldment of the sense of service in the future.
  E. Application of the concept of service to our modern educational developments.

Training for new age
discipleship is provided
by the *Arcane School*.
The principles of the
Ageless Wisdom are
presented through esoteric
meditation, study and
service as a *way of life*.

*Write to the publishers
for information.*

INDEX

Abstract thinking, need for, 145
Adolescents, education. *See* Education of adolescents.
Adult education. *See* Education, adult.
Age—
  Aquarian. *See* Aquarian Age.
  of synthesis, 3
  Piscean. *See* Piscean Age.
  See also Children, age.
Alignment of—
  mind and brain, 6
  soul, mind, and brain, 50–51
Ambition, breeding, 105
America, contribution to unfoldment, 50
Angel, Solar—
  definition, 5
  manifestation, 141
  relation to personality, 148
  See also Soul.
Animal kingdom, relation of man to, 126
Antahkarana—
  anchor, 31, 32
  and sutratma, use as unit, 31
  bridging factors, 126
  building—
    beginning, 29, 31
    by race, 94
    first half, 96, 97
    means, 6, 27
    methods, 2
    results, 95–96
    second half, 96–97
  comparison with sutratma, 26–27
  connection with Great White Lodge, 52
  continuity of consciousness, 26, 31
  definitions, 6, 26, 27
  expression, 52
  extension, 28, 148
  functions, 2, 26, 28, 52, 146, 148
  group, 29
  inter-weaving with sutratma, 28
  links, 33
  recognition, 146
  relation to light, 52
  Science of. *See* Science of Antahkarana.

symbolism, 7
use, 28, 146
world, 131
See also Bridge; Thread, consciousness.
Aquarian—
  Age—
    education. *See* Education.
    incidence and characteristics, 121–125
    Noble Middle Path, 42
    type of idealist, contrast with Piscean, 122
Archetypes. *See* Patterns.
Architect, production, 113
Arithmetic, symbolism, 15–16
Art, creative activity, 17–18
Artist, production, 113
Arts—
  creative, production, 20–21
  renaissance, preparation for, 47
Aryan race, unfoldment, triple, 50–51
Aryans, light, attainment, 54
"As a man thinketh, so is he," 2
Asia—
  contribution to unfoldment of Aryan race, 50
  education, results, 79
Aspects—
  consciousness, anchorage in man, 92
  consciousness in child, reorientation, 93
  life or spirit, anchorage in man, 92
  soul, concern of esotericism, 67
  soul, evocation upon physical plane, 19–20
  third, forces, reception of energies, 67
Aspirants—
  building antahkarana, 31, 146
  goal, 146
  use of sutratma, 30–31
Astral body. *See* Body, astral.
Astrology—
  esoteric, facts, recognition and use, 70–71
  modern ordinary, superseding, 71
  use in education, 10, 51, 72

155

Service—Continued
vocational, in adolescence, 89
See also Science of service.
Sex—
expression of universe, 137
hygiene, errors, 136
hygiene, growth, 136
life, regulation, 136
magic, error, 137
physiological processes, need for, 137
problem, relation to Hierarchy, 132
problem, relation to parenthood, 131–132
relation, information, implications, 137
relation, objective, 137–138
Sexes, relationships, mentally controlled, 136
Sexual—
control, lack, result, 135
promiscuity, cessation, 135
Shamballa, emanations, 140
Silver cord. *See* Sutratma.
Simplicity of living, return to, 121
Social—
consciousness, cultivation, 35
order, participation in Plan, 56
organisation, teaching, 84, 88
Solar plexus centre. *See* Centre, solar plexus.
Son of God, appearance as light, 137
Sorrow, value, educational, 120
Soul—
activity, factors, 19
age, study, 11
and its mechanism, fusion, 33
and personality, bridge between, building and results, 95
and personality, bridge between, building, means, 96
and Spiritual Triad, bridge between, building, results, 26, 95
aspects, evocation upon physical plane, 19–21
at-one-ment with personality, 35
attribute, element in service, 97
attributes, evocation upon physical plane, 19, 21–23
bridging with Monad and personality, 145
characteristic, major, 144
consciousness in children, 76–77
contact, leaders possessing, work, 117–118
contact, results, 141

creation of antahkarana, 148
creation of forms, 20–21
creative power, means, 18
definitions, 5, 19
discovery in oneself, results, 29
energies from higher mental levels, sensitivity to, 61
energy, anchor, 31
functions on three lower planes, 36
fusion with personality, 136–137, 141
individual, awakening, 105–106
individual, status, 126
indwelling, manifestation, 141
knowledge, anchorage in body, 92
knowledge, faculty, 92
life, response to, training, 19
linking with personality, result, 97
misconception, recognition in education, 25
mystical vision of, 113
of all things, definition, 64
of humanity, awakening *en masse,* 106–107
powers, unfoldment, seven methods, 19–24
purpose, allegiance to, 22
purpose, indication, 71
relation to—
antahkarana, 145, 146, 148
personality, 137
Spiritual Triad, 31
the good, true, and beautiful, 86
response to, registration, 12
studies, 9
synonyms, 5
union with, urge, cause, 21
vehicle. *See* Body, light.
world—
activity, 148
mediation, 67
relation to atoms, 148
See also Ego.
Souls—
achievement of perfection, 134
incarnating, bodies for, provision, 137
kingdom of. *See* Kingdom of souls.
world of, bridging with world of phenomena, 145
world of, relation of human being to, teaching, 49
Source, return of man to, 21
Spider symbol, 32
Spirit in manifestation, 63